PASSAGE INTO DISCIPLESHIP

I dedicate this book to Jennifer, my wife,
for her loving support and encouragement to complete this project.
I also dedicate this book to my children,
Sara and Walker, who remind me of the childlike qualities
that teach us adults about faith in God.

PASSAGE INTO DISCIPLESHIP
Guide to Baptism

Christopher W. Wilson

CHALICE
PRESS
ST. LOUIS, MISSOURI

Cover image from a photo by: Martin Barraud/OJO Images/GettyImages
Cover and interior design: Elizabeth Wright

Visit Chalice Press on the World Wide Web at
www.chalicepress.com

10 9 8 7 6 5 4 3 2 1   09 10 11 12 13 14 15 16

EPUB ISBN: 978-08272-30149 • EPDF ISBN: 978-08272-30156

Library of Congress Cataloging–in–Publication Data
Wilson, Christopher W. (Christopher Walker)
 Passage into discipleship : guide to baptism / by Christopher W. Wilson.
   p. cm.
 ISBN 978-0-8272-3008-8
 1. Christian education of children—Study and teaching. 2. Baptism—Study and teaching. I. Title.

 BV1475.3.W56 2009
 268'.433—dc22

                                                    2009024089

Printed in the United States of America

Contents

Acknowledgments

I would like to acknowledge several people and churches that helped me reach the point of writing and sharing the content of this publication.

I want to acknowledge the late Dr. Kenneth Lawrence for his constant support of my education in knowing personality development and learning theory for congregational life. I also want to thank Dr. J. Cy Rowell, whose dedication to Christian education in the local church has inspired me to create meaningful experiences and liturgy for the church. It is with his encouragement that I share the content of this book with other congregations.

I want to thank the following congregations for allowing me to share various forms of this publication's content in guiding people toward baptism and the continued Christian life that baptism brings:

Ridglea Christian Church of Fort Worth, Texas
River Oaks Christian Church of Fort Worth, Texas
Los Altos Christian Church of Albuquerque, New Mexico
Rush Creek Christian Church of Arlington, Texas

These congregations provided a healthy environment for youth to grow in their faith and in the Christian community.

I want to thank *Make It Clear Ministries* for permission to use the spiritual gift inventory. They wrote a helpful gift exercise appropriate for the age I target in this book.

Last, I want to give thanks to Martha Schooley for her reading and reflections during the writing process.

Introduction

One of the most exciting moments for me as a minister is when a young person approaches me and shares the desire to be baptized. I am thrilled when a young person wants to learn more, grow more, and embrace fully the Christian faith. Baptism is a significant moment in any person's life.

I remember when Holly walked up to me in the halls of the church one Sunday morning. She tugged on my shirt. I turned my head to find Holly with an eager face ready to talk. She said, "I think I'm ready." "What are you ready for?" I asked. "I still have a lot of questions about God and the church, but in my heart I want to be baptized and follow Jesus." All it takes is a nudge in our spirits to enter us into a new world. Holly went through the process I am proposing in this book. The day of her baptism was a true celebration. She began to make her way into the baptistry. I could tell she was nervous by the way she grasped my hand as I guided her down the steps. I introduced her and her family to the church and celebrated her confession of faith made the week before. I placed my hand on her head and blessed her. I slowly lowered her into the water and raised her back out. As soon as she wiped the water from her face, a huge smile appeared. The fear was gone and the joy filled her being. I said to her, "Holly, I want to welcome you to the family of God on behalf of the universal church. Today, you are a new creation in Christ." The congregation had watched Holly grow up in the church. Her baptism marked a new chapter in her life. It was a few weeks after that glorious day when I felt a tap on my shoulder. It was Holly. She had a calm sweet smile on her face and simply said, "Thanks." Her passage into discipleship had begun.

I encounter too many Christians who have little memory of their baptismal process. They might recall being baptized, but do not remember how they were nurtured toward their baptism. This is a tragedy for the church. We need to be able to recall and remember our baptism and what led up to it. *Passage into Discipleship: Guide to Baptism* is a book seeking to prepare young people not only for their baptisms but for the Christian journey that follows. It is helpful to know baptism is not a static moment in time. Baptism has claim on us for the remainder of our Christian lives. The title of this book implies entry into an active life with Christ.

2 Passage into Discipleship

Passage into Discipleship: Guide to Baptism is the result of many years of working with young people with a desire to know Christ more fully through the act of baptism. Early in my ministry, I had a hard time finding what I was looking for in a preparation process. I could not find resources that encompassed all I wanted to accomplish in preparing young people for baptism. I began writing my own curriculum and structure. This publication is a result of over ten years of exploring what did and did not work well. It is my hope that you will find *Passage into Discipleship* to be a helpful resource in guiding young people in their faith and in preparing them for baptism.

This book is intended primarily for students from approximately fourth through seventh grades. The content and structure relate to the spiritual and mental development of that age range. The intent is to use learning methods that best instill memory and retention about key theological and biblical concepts. The main audience for this book is leaders who educate youth in a believer's baptism tradition. The content of this book can also be used by denominations that practice infant baptism and confirmation. Confirmation occurs at a similar age to when we practice believer's baptism. The substance is applicable to a confirmation tradition. The goal is guiding young people to embrace a journey of faith with Jesus Christ.

Every Christian can recall or claim particular moments, experiences, people, and places that shaped their faith. My desire is to offer a process for young people so they can look back to their baptismal preparation and baptism as one of the most meaningful and moving times in their Christian journey. It is my hope they will not look back upon their baptism as a faint memory, but rather as a vital time that encouraged them to grow deeper in faith and seek lives of hope as faithful followers of Jesus Christ.

This publication offers a new and comprehensive approach to guiding people to and beyond their baptism. A former model for preparing young people for baptism involved meeting with the minister a few times to learn what baptism meant. The person was baptized once those few discussions were completed. This method was not wrong or without integrity or great intention. The idea was to ensure young persons knew what they were doing before the act of baptism was complete. This process may have led them to know what baptism "meant," as if it were a subject taught in school. The process I am introducing attempts to engage the minds, hearts, and souls of young people. I want them not only to grasp the meaning of baptism, but to embrace the Christian journey knowing baptism is their entry into a glorious life with God and other Christians. I want them to know baptism is an event that will continue to shape them throughout their lives. It is a process of discipleship and joining others in this quest to be faithful Christians together. Many of us have heard the liturgical phrase, "Remember your baptism and be glad." May the young people that benefit from this process remember their baptismal process as a time of confirmation in which God was active and alive in their lives.

Teaching about baptism and the Christian life should instill excitement and curiosity in young people. They are at an age with lots of questions. Youth not only hunger for knowledge, they hunger for inclusion and love. The hope is to encourage the whole church to celebrate their passage toward the baptismal waters. We are to have a covenantal relationship with any person seeking to be baptized into the Christian community. This is particularly true for the young people who will shape and give life to the future of our church.

This book is intended for ministers and other church leaders who will lead youth through the preparation process for baptism and the journey of the Christian life. The content is a multidimensional approach, inviting youth to learn the material in multiple ways. Appendices at the end of the book contain class outlines, worksheets, and other helpful materials. Please review the material in the appendices so you are fully aware of the content to aid you in the overall conducting of the process. The appendicies may be photocopied or downloaded from www.chalicepress.com for use with this book.

The desire to write this material is a desire for churches to provide a process for our youth to embrace the moment of baptism and the ongoing claim it has upon our lives. Baptism welcomes us into the family of God as newly cleansed and renewed persons in body, mind, and spirit. My expectation is for youth, once baptized, to enter the full life of the church beyond the youth group. They will have been exposed to all facets of the church, its beliefs, and its mission outside the walls of the church, while remembering it is all because we seek to know and honor God with our blessed lives.

You never know when a Holly will tug on your shirt and inquire about baptism. The church should be ready with a process to guide students to live in the Christian faith after they are baptized. Let God bless each of you in the work you do to serve the church of Jesus Christ.

Rationale

Why Are We Baptizing?

Through the baptismal process, a person enters into the Christian faith blessed and strengthened by God. They also enter into the life of the church to express faith in the midst of a wider Christian community. Baptism is about building up the body of Christ. Each time a person enters into the fold, the church expands and is enriched. The church is about relationships and working together in Christ's name. The church is not a place of individuals with a disconnected purpose. Unity in Christ is a guiding principle that connects Christians to one another in the midst of our diversity of gifts and abilities. We are baptizing people to enter into eternal life with God and a committed life to Christ's church as a people of faith.

Developmental Assessment

I believe it is important to know who we are teaching and guiding in order to maximize the learning experience. The material in this book targets young people between the fourth and seventh grades. There is some flexibility on either side, depending on the development of a particular person.

I try to imagine the person who will be attending the sessions I am teaching. This is the kind of young person I imagine walking in the door:

- Begins to identify with Jesus in a personal way and begins to ask religious questions
- Senses the love and support of a Christian community
- Wants to act with justice and to be fair with others
- Has a high level of respect for ministers and teachers
- Is beginning to move beyond concrete thinking into some abstract thinking
- Enjoys the value of friendship and working with others
- Beginning to develop convictions about what she believes is right and wrong
- Values his parent(s)/caregivers and is starting to add value from what his peers share

- Is eager to be accepted and included by others
- Can begin to take concepts and apply them to her personal life
- Finds joy in working and exploring areas of interest
- Is filled with great creativity and enjoys interactive processes

These qualities are indicative of the kind of youth that entertain thoughts about baptism. They are at a transition time in their spiritual, moral, relational, and mental development. Curiosity is at an all-time high. The preparation process for baptism is important to capture much of what they are going through developmentally. The material should be supportive of this stage of development for these young people.

Passage into Discipleship seeks to get the most out of the youth by providing discussion and activities matching where they are in their faith development. Youth are to be challenged and engaged without having to remember too much theory. Instruction is to be balanced with left and right brain approaches. The content of this book balances theology and ideas with interactive exercises and experiences.

Learning Theory

This book is a multidimensional learning approach. Youth learn from different methods of teaching. This book's process includes four learning theories that overlap one another. One reason for this approach is to make sure all the youth learn the concepts and content conveyed, since different models work for different people. Another reason is to reinforce what they learn through more than one learning model. They will get the same material taught in different formats.

The traditional model of classroom teaching is still valid, but needs to be surrounded by other models to capture the minds of youth. The process of baptism preparation is not about reciting the right answers, but rather aiding them in exploring the Christian faith and how they will express and share that faith in Christ's name.

What do we know about older children and youth in terms of learning techniques? In her book *Transforming Bible Study with Children: A Guide for Learning Together,* Patricia W. Van Ness argues that children and youth targeted at the age of this book learn through personal experience much more so than through words and classic classroom instruction. This does not mean we should not include this style of teaching, but we should be aware of additional models that encourage greater memory and engagement. Van Ness includes in her book a diagram by Arlen Ban, which states that young people remember 10 percent of things we tell them with words while they remember 90 percent of things they do. The 10 percent is when the learner is listening only. The 90 percent is when the learner is actively involved. And young people remember 60 percent when the learner has something to see.[1] All this data tells us we ought to be including in our learning processes as many experience-based opportunities as possible. This will yield the greatest chance for remembering what we teach them.

To make the point stronger Van Ness utilizes another diagram by Edgar Dale called Dale's Cone of Learning. This diagram shows 10 degrees of effectiveness in learning for children. Number ten, or the least effective means of learning, is words. The most effective is direct, purposeful, personal experience. Adults are so concerned about the words with which we teach, yet Dale reminds us that this is the least effective practice for teaching children.[2] Van Ness argues that we as Christian teachers should be transforming our models of teaching to engage and inspire youth in the learning process.[3] We are invited to combine experiences and words to take full advantage of the learning that is possible with a young person.

The content and approach of learning includes four models to reinforce and strengthen the experience base for teaching youth interested in baptism. The four learning models are:

- Instructional sessions: Classes teaching basic Christian concepts, theological beliefs, scriptural knowledge, and methods of prayer
- Experience-based sessions: Living out what was learned in the instructional sessions
- One-on-one relationships: Forming a mentor relationship with a leader in the church to teach similar concepts taught in the instructional and experiential sessions
- Retreat format: A full day of experiences that could not be accomplished in a smaller one-to-two-hour session; provides a way to build relationships with other youth and leaders in the church by sharing common excursions and experiences of expressing faith.

Three of these four models are experience-based. The instructional model still exists to communicate language and concepts to provide a base of knowledge for what youth experience in other parts of the learning process.

---

[1]Patricia W. Van Ness, *Transforming Bible Study with Children: A Guide for Learning Together* (Nashville: Abingdon Press, 1991), 23.

[2]Ibid., 24.

[3]Ibid., 26.

John Westerhoff reminds us, "Together children, youth, and adults must have an opportunity to experience the activity of the people of God and become involved in the reflective action of the community of faith. Only then can we call the church an educating community."[4] He goes on to say that relevant church education is found with congregations who are serious about the role of experience in the lives of youth.[5] Youth who encounter this type of learning will grow exponentially compared to those taught by methods that do not include a high number of experiences for them. It is important to know who you are teaching in order to provide the best method for assimilation and growth in the learner.

It has been my experience in teaching youth who previously participated in the process that they recall the experiences before they remember any classroom sessions. If they can remember the experiences and what they were intended to accomplish, then the content of the classroom sessions will be retrieved from their minds much easier. It makes sense that even though we teach classroom first and then practice what we learn, the youth remember the practice before the instruction. This strengthens the argument for greater attention being given to experience-oriented learning combined with classroom-oriented learning, rather than exclusively using classroom learning. The more ways we can stimulate the minds of young people the greater the retention becomes.

The Power of Memory

I have already highlighted a primary way that memory is instilled in the youth who go through this program: through the combination of learning approaches being used to teach the same content. Youth are being taught similar Christian themes in four different ways. This style of teaching reinforces what they are learning by how they are learning.

The other part of developing memory and the remembrance of what they learn is through alliteration. All of the basic concepts taught begin with the letter "c." It is much easier to remember basic concepts through memory techniques. If I know that what I am learning follows a pattern, then I am much more likely to remember a pattern if it exists. There is simplicity to the themes even though they communicate a rich relevance to the Christian faith. The "c" words I teach are:

---

[4]John H. Westerhoff III, *Values for Tomorrow's Children: An Alternative Future for Education in the Church* (New York: Pilgrim Press, 1979), 45.
[5]Ibid., 79.

- *Confession:* What we believe
- *Contrition:* Restoring relationship with God
- *Covenant:* Holy moments with God through Christ
- *Community:* Strengthening the church and serving the world
- *Connection:* Discovering our spiritual gifts and how they are used with the gifts of others
- *Church:* What is the purpose of our being together in Christ's name?

The multiple learning styles, combined with the use of alliterative language, create powerful memories. The hope is that, years from now, the youth could look back upon their baptisms and the process of preparing for those baptisms and remember events, classes, and a congregation that supported them in their faith journey to serve Jesus Christ and the church.

Theological Approach

What are the theological foundations of *Passage into Discipleship*? The theological approach communicates three main ideas with the youth. The first one is that they are an important part of the body of Christ as manifested in the church. The second idea is that baptism is not a destination, but part of a longer journey with God and other Christians. The third foundation is celebrating the young people as a special and unique part of God's creation in the human family.

Youth are often told they are the future of the church, yet they are part of the church right now. Sometimes youth do not know how important they are to the church, which hopefully will change through this process. Youth can be actively involved in church life if given the opportunity to serve. They have gifts and abilities like everyone else. Each youth needs to hear the church say they are an important part of the church family.

I remind youth going through the class that the desired result of the classes is not baptism. If they *choose* to be baptized in the end, it is a celebration for them, their families, and the church. I tell them they are beginning a journey of faith with God that will unfold throughout their lives. Baptism is a way to formally seal their love of God and Christ. Baptism enters us into eternal life with God, but it should not mean we are finished growing and developing as persons of faith. Baptism should compel us to learn more and be open to how God might use us in the world.

Youth need to be affirmed for who they are. They need to feel more confident in how God made them. We so easily compare ourselves to others and may look down on ourselves. God believes in each of us. We were created for a purpose. We all have something to offer this world. Youth need to learn early how important they are and that God loves them for who they are. The whole process is a guide in discipleship and baptism, and it is also a way to develop a more confident and mature young person.

Baptism Training as a Faith Community

Ministers historically have been the sole teachers of youth preparing for baptism. It is my desire to create an intergenerational environment for young people. The inclusion of mentors, parents, and other church leaders is designed to nurture relationships for youth beyond the youth group. Churches tend to congregate in age groups. Youth gravitate toward youth. We can best integrate youth into the full life of the church if they develop meaningful relationships with adults in the church. Then they will be more inclined to talk and participate in events beyond youth functions.

The church's role in guiding youth to baptism is a congregational role and not one reserved exclusively for the minister. Expanding the responsibility for baptism to the whole church invites more involvement from the church membership. The hope is to change the title of preparing youth for baptism from the "Pastor's Class" to more of a "Discipleship Class," which implies greater involvement from the church community.

Discipleship Process Overview

If more people are going to be involved, then it is important to know where they can be involved. It might be helpful to visualize the three primary parts of the discipleship program for youth.

Class Component

Session 1	Orientation with Youth and Parents
Session 2	Confession (classroom)
Session 3	Confession (experience)
Session 4	Contrition (classroom)
Session 5	Contrition (experience)
Session 6	Covenant (classroom)
Session 7	Covenant (experience)
Session 8	Community (classroom)
Session 9	Community (experience)
Session 10	Connection (classroom)
Session 11	Connection (experience)
Session 12	Church (classroom)

Mentor Component

- Each youth is connected with a mentor for the duration of the class sessions.
- The mentor and youth have continual things and one-time projects to accomplish together.
- The mentors will provide insights about their journeys of faith and connection to the church not covered in the class sessions and relate those insights to the subject being learned in the sessions above.

Day Retreat Component

- The day retreat has three components
  —Human-Creation relationship: go to a creation setting
  —Human-Human relationship: care project for others
  —Human-God relationship: prayer/worship experience
- The purpose is to understand the above three primary ways we relate in the world.
- The retreat is intended to come at the end of the twelve class sessions.
- The church leadership can recruit people to help with class sessions, be open to mentoring youth, help coordinate events for group outings, and encourage congregational members to talk and ask questions of the youth going through the process. Invite all to share what they are learning and what they enjoy about the process.

Adapting to Church Size

How can this material be used in churches of different sizes? The key is training staff and members of the church to be leaders of the process regardless of the size.

Smaller Churches

Smaller church may have less youth going through the process. In this case give additional strength to the mentor component of the program. The minister or key leaders of the sessions can give greater attention to a small number of youth than a large number. Invite more participation from the congregation in surrounding this youth with support, encouragement, and intergenerational activities.

Larger Churches

Larger congregations will need to train additional congregational members/leaders to assist with class sessions and group outings. Leadership teams will need to be in touch before each session to lead sessions with a common understanding and approach for the youth. Larger churches might need to be creative with youth/mentor shadowing. Be sure to check with worship planning and service logistics to ensure a smooth experience for the mentors guiding youth in worship.

Adding a Creative Edge

I always welcome creative ideas and thoughts from others as they read a book or reflect on curriculum material. I encourage you to consider ways to add your own identity to the work presented in this publication. There may be other exercises or games that could strengthen a session. The use of technology can be a great benefit. I encourage the support of the material in this book by watching movies or video clips, using Christian or secular music, or even inviting youth to interact with certain Web sites if you think it would be helpful. The overall goal is to reach into the minds and hearts of the young people we are guiding.

Logistics

It is always important to protect the youth anytime they are the focus of an activity. The church should do background checks on any adult directly involved with a youth. This would be true for any teachers of class sessions as well as mentors. The last thing you want is to have an adult that would be a danger to the process.

Most churches have permission forms for youth to travel as a group beyond the church facility for an event. Since the program calls for several experience sessions away from the church, it is important for parents to complete these forms before any traveling occurs.

Recruit parents or congregational members to assist with transportation needs. Those offering to help with rides can also serve as additional adult supervision. Leaders of sessions will be hindered if they have not pre-planned transportation logistics.

Have a backup plan. If something you coordinate does not work out as anticipated, then have an alternative activity ready to go. Our best plans do not always unfold the way we imagined.

Opportunity for the Minister

The minister's involvement and leadership in this process create an excellent opportunity to make connections with the youth in the church. The shared classes and experiences provide a concentrated time with the youth a minister rarely has. This is important in creating an environment for the minister to connect with people of all ages in the congregation. This class has affforded me a way to create healthy bonds with the youth of the church, which allows me to develop a continued relationship with them for years to come. A minister is not always able to attend and participate in all the youth functions. The preparation process for baptism opens a doorway of connection to youth that might otherwise be limited.

Class Component

Session 1   **Orientation**

Session 2   **Confession** (classroom)

Session 3   **Confession** (experience)

Session 4   **Contrition** (classroom)

Session 5   **Contrition** (experience)

Session 6   **Covenant** (classroom)

Session 7   **Covenant** (experience)

Session 8   **Community** (classroom)

Session 9   **Community** (experience)

Session 10   **Connection** (classroom)

Session 11   **Connection** (experience)

Session 12   **Church**

SESSION 1: Orientation

Getting Oriented

The orientation session with youth and parents helps each family learn about the discipleship and baptism process. Promote the baptism process through newsletters, phone calls, or face-to-face interactions. Invite the youth and their parents so both hear about the details of the process and what is expected of each person who wants to participate. The orientation session is to be led with excitement to highlight the joy of these young people who are interested in becoming more faithful in their lives as followers of Jesus Christ.

The orientation is an overview of all that the youth will encounter in the weekly sessions, in the interaction with mentors, and in a closing retreat. The purpose is creating an environment with various learning approaches to best help a young person grow in his or her Christian faith. The process includes four learning approaches: (1) class instruction, (2) experience instruction, (3) mentor instruction, and (4) closing retreat. The design is to reinforce and build on the content and learning covered throughout the process. Distribute the overview sheet that shows how the different components are scheduled. This allows the youth and parents to see that classroom sessions are a combination of instruction and experience. The purpose is to practice what they learn the week before. Mention that many of the classroom sessions include a worksheet or activity that is to be completed before the youth return for the next session. Encourage parents to work with their children in completing assignments. The completed assignment provides the best preparation for the next week.

The process is intended to inform youth about the covenantal nature of our faith. We rely on God to guide us and love us, and God relies on us to become faithful followers. The draw to the process is to discern about baptism, but it should not be an expected outcome. If any youth reach the end of the process and do not feel ready, then they can wait to be baptized at another time. I have had the experience of youth deciding to wait rather than feel the peer pressure to be baptized because everyone else is being baptized. The process is about becoming and continuing to be faithful followers of Jesus and disciples of Christ.

The mentor selection is very important for the youth. The youth will be asked to submit three names of church leaders of the same gender they would like as mentors. You will make the contacts. When their mentor is confirmed, you notify the youth. The mentor process begins once this pairing is accomplished. Mentors will be given clear instructions of activities and material to complete with you.

The closing retreat will be a day you will all share together, which allows you to experience three distinct areas of learning that you are covering in small ways throughout the class. It is a day of fun and growth for everyone.

Remind the parents that full participation of their children ensures the best overall experience. Also remind them to stay involved with what the youth are learning and share the journey with their children. Parents may be called on to help with transportation and help with the experience sessions of the process. This includes help with the retreat day.

Allow time at the end for youth and parents to ask questions. Questions help give clarity to anything you might have failed to mention or cover.

The final part of the orientation is deciding on the best time for the group to meet weekly. I have found that different groups often have different optimal times to meet during the week. Work with your group, for you want to ensure as full attendance as possible.

Remember to begin and end the orientation with prayer for these young people who are interested in baptism and becoming more familiar with being faithful followers of Jesus.

The materials you will need for the orientation are the outline and the overview sheets found in appendix A.

SESSION 2: Confession
(classroom)

Theme: Confession

Class Concepts

- Confession as a belief statement
- Confession as the moment we write or say what we believe to others
- We should not be afraid to share with others what we believe
- We learn from scripture that followers of Jesus had to decide for themselves what they believed about Jesus

Scripture Emphasis: Matthew 16:13–20

Theological Foundation

- This session helps youth develop a credo (personal faith construction) that will help them in their Christian journey
- What we believe and communicate about God, Christ, and church is an important step in developing our foundation of faith
- An important part of our Christian identity comes in sharing the gospel message with others (as commanded in the great commission in Matthew 28:18–20)

Class Outline for Leaders

Opening Prayer

Sentence Completion Exercise

The first exercise consists of completing sentences. Share with the group that God created us all. Each person is special and unique. Share more about yourself with the youth by completing the following statements seen below.

17

Then have each of the youth complete the same statements. An easy way to begin the confessional process is by sharing basic information. Once everyone feels comfortable and safe, the conversations will open up to sharing deeper faith beliefs. There are no right or wrong responses to the uncompleted sentences.

- My name is…
- I was born…
- Three words that describe me are…
- Something important to me is…
- I am involved in the church because…
- I am in this class because…

Bragging Exercise

The next exercise is a "bragging" session. You will want a stopwatch or other watch to keep track of time. Each person will have two minutes to share as much about him- or herself as possible with the group. Each person can share freely and name the following kinds of things: family details; hobbies or personal interests; favorite movie, music, food, color, etc.; specials talents; and what is unique about him- or herself. You might discover that the youth have a hard time filling the two minutes talking about themselves. Speaking out loud about ourselves can be harder than we realize when we are the center of attention. More extroverted youth will do better with this activity and it will challenge others to expand their comfort zones.

What Is Confession?

Discuss what the word *confession* means. First, ask the class members what they think the word means. After the group has shared their responses, teach two ways that *confession* may be understood. One definition is that it is the act of telling another person or God that you are sorry for something that has happened. A second definition is that it is an oral or written statement of belief, which is what this session is all about.

Scripture Discussion

When focusing on confession as a statement of belief, the participants are going to put this into action. Read Matthew 16:13–20. Jesus was learning what the disciples were hearing about him and also what his followers were thinking of him. Discuss the difference between saying what others believe and what one personally believes. The community of believers around us shapes our faith, but we must come to terms with what we ourselves believe. Our confessions can tell us about our priorities in life and how we see and experience the world around us. Confession is when we own what we say to others and ourselves.

When we say or write what we believe, then it becomes a confession. Ideas and thoughts need to be articulated and brought out into the open through sharing. Confession occurs when God and others know what it is that we believe. Young people are often instructed to recite back what is taught to them. Confession is more than reciting what we are told to believe. Confession is investing our lives in what we feel is important to us and how we should live our lives. This kind of confession helps shape our identity and enables us to relate to others in our world—to people who believe in similar or different ways.

It is important for Christians to know what they believe and be willing to share that belief with others. It is important to be proud of our belief system and be confident in why we believe it.

Other Christians' Confessions

Have the youth look in the *Chalice Hymnal* at examples of what other Christians have said about their faith and church throughout Christian history.

- A Disciples Affirmation (no. 355)
- Nicene Affirmation of Faith (no. 358)
- Apostolic Affirmation of Faith (no. 359)
- United Church of Christ Statement of Faith (no. 361)

Ask the group to share what they see as common threads among all the statements of faith. What is unique about some of the statements? Remind the class that each statement is a way for a community of faith to express what they believe as Christians. (If you do not have access to the *Chalice Hymnal,* then you can find these and similar statements in denominational resources or on the Internet.)

First Person Exercise

The next activity is called "First Person Exercise." Split into three groups, dividing up as evenly as possible. Each group will take on a faith entity and share with the rest of the class who they are and why they are important. The groups will take on the following entities: God, Jesus Christ, and Church. They must use "I" statements to share who they are.

Here is an example. If there are six youth in the class, divide the class into three groups of two. One set of two people will be assigned "God." They will write up to five sentences starting with "I" without using the word *God*. The statements should describe God or God's actions and give clues for the other class participants to guess who they are describing. The other sets of two youth will do the same for Jesus Christ and the Church.

The hope is for the youth to better understand the nature and function of God, Jesus Christ, and the Church by using language to characterize them. It is one thing to believe in God, and quite another to describe God to another person.

Confession Exercise Worksheet

In concluding the session, pass out the worksheet for the Confession Exercise found in appendix C. The students are to write what they believe about the three words listed on the page in sentences, phrases, words, or images. They are to bring the confession worksheets back for the next session.

Closing Prayer

Close the session with a prayer that allows the youth to share something with God that they are thankful for in their lives.

Supplies Needed

- Copies of the session outline to hand out at the beginning of your time together (see appendix B) or write the outline on a board or paper for all to see
- Pencils/pens and paper for the class members to take notes
- Bibles for all class members for the scripture discussion
- Hymnals or other copies of creeds for all class members when discussing historical confession statements
- Stopwatch or watch for "bragging session" exercise
- Confession Exercise worksheet to pass out at the close of the session

"Confession is investing our lives in what we feel is important to us and how we should live our lives."

SESSION 3: Confession
(experiential)

Open the session with a prayer.

Tell the youth they are going on a field trip, but do not tell them where they are going. They need to bring the Confession Exercise worksheet they completed during the week.

Take the youth to a site that is away from people. Go outside the city limits or to a remote place in the city or community in which you live. Once there, you will invite each youth to shout two things. First, they are to shout something they do or like ("I like baseball"; "I like dancing"; etc.). Second, they are to shout out a sentence or phrase from their confession sheets. They will do this one person at a time. If they are not very loud, then encourage them to be as loud as possible. Remind them there is no one around.

After this exercise is done, you will then take them to a second destination that will be a surprise to the youth. One idea is to take them to a parking lot where there are a good number of people around, such as at a grocery store or mall. If you take them *inside* of a store or mall, make sure you have permission from the management. Invite them to go through the same exercise as they did at the remote location. Encourage them to be as loud as possible, knowing they will probably be much quieter than they were previously.

After they are finished, go back to the church to talk about their experience. Have the class members share what it was like at the remote site. The following questions are some ideas of how to begin the discussion. Was there a difference for them in shouting a simple statement of what they like compared to a belief statement? What was it like for them to shout out loud something they believe? Did they feel safe knowing no one was around? Was it hard or easy to do? Have they ever done anything like that before?

Next, talk about the parking lot experience. Discuss why it was more difficult than at the first location. Talk about the importance of being proud of the faith they have in God and Jesus Christ. Let them know they are not to be ashamed of sharing their faith with others. They will not go around shouting, but they should be confident enough to share what is important to them regardless of what others think.

This is a good time to talk about how we share our faith with those who practice no faith or are a part of another faith tradition. Confession is not meant to be judging or condemning in any way. Confession is a way to be in dialogue with others about what is vital and important to us. When we share our faith with confidence, we demonstrate the importance of the Christian faith to those not a part of the church. However, we are to be respectful of others and what they believe.

Confession allows us to be in honest dialogue with others whose beliefs are different from ours. If we share our faith with integrity and assurance, we enhance the chances that another person will be more interested in what we believe.

Close the session with a prayer.

*"It is important to be honest with God in
how we live out our faith toward
God and one another."*

SESSION 4: Contrition
(CLASSROOM)

Theme: Contrition

Class Concepts:

- How to grow closer to God
- Repentance is a choice we make about changing attitudes and actions in being faithful to God and others
- The role of repentance as Jesus Christ urges us down a new path from the one we were on before
- Forgiveness is learning that we rely on God and others to mend relationships that are broken
- Forgiveness does not imply that we forget what we have done or what others have done in the fracturing of relationships, but is it about finding new ways to heal those relationships

Scripture Emphasis: Acts 9:1–19

Theological Foundation

- Repentance and forgiveness are characteristics of the Christian way of life
- Repentance and forgiveness acknowledge a humility and dependence on God to help make our lives whole
- How we relate to God is a model for how we relate to others in the world (people of all faith traditions)
- God invites humanity to seek healthy and whole paths in faith rather than contradicting the unity God desires for all of us

Class Outline for Leader

Opening Prayer

Chocolate Chip Cookie Exercise

Hand each young person a chocolate chip cookie. Tell the youth not to eat the cookies, but rather to wait for instructions on what to do with them. Make sure everyone has a cookie and a napkin. The youth are to put the napkins on the tables in front of them. Next, each youth is encouraged to attempt to pull out the chocolate chips without destroying the cookie. Give them a few minutes to try this activity. They will quickly realize that they cannot get the chocolate chips out and not destroy the cookie.

Use this exercise to explain to them that our faith is a vital part of our lives. When our faith in God is not right, it has effects on the rest of our lives, too. Our faith influences our attitudes, our relationships with others, our values and morals, and our actions. God wants us to be whole and to establish a faith that creates a foundation that will not crumble. We can all do things in our lives that can create pain, struggle, and hardship, yet God wants us to choose a path that is intended to generate love, peace, unity, and community.

Scripture Discussion

Invite the youth to open their Bibles to Acts 9:1–19. This is the story of Saul of Tarsus, who eventually becomes Paul. The resurrected Christ encounters Saul and helps him establish a life that honors God and is modeled after Jesus Christ. Saul goes through a radical change. He goes from killing and arresting Christians to advocating for the Christian life and establishing churches. The presence of Christ in our lives can urge and call us to a new way of living. Saul becomes a changed man the day he encountered Christ. When we make the choice to follow Jesus Christ, we begin a journey that includes growth, new beginnings, grace, and forgiveness. We cannot be, nor should we imagine ourselves to be, perfect as Christians, but we are called to be faithful and seek a meaningful and close relationship with God.

What was it that caused Paul to change? Paul's change began by the risen Christ initiating a relationship with him. Paul's encounter with Christ made him realize what he was doing to hurt those who loved God. Christ thrusted Paul into a discernment period via Paul's loss of sight. He had to pause in the midst of his life and reflect on what Christ said to him. Did Paul go through this change in his life alone? How do our lives become better with God?

What Is Sin?

What is sin? There are many ways to define or talk about sin with young people. We often make the mistake and talk about *sins* with a small "s," rather than talking about *Sin* with a big "S." Sin is primarily how we distance ourselves from God's presence in intentional and unintentional ways. Even though we are intended for good as God created us, we are not perfect and fall short of what God expects of us. Below is a list of ways to help youth understand the nature of sin.

- Sin is things we do that are harmful to our relationship with God
- Sin is things we do that are harmful to ourselves or others and that we knowingly do
- Sin is things we do that are harmful to ourselves or others that we do not knowingly do
- Sin is failing to respond to others with our love and compassion
- Sin happens with individuals and communities

The human journey is to move closer to God. Draw pictures of the diagrams below to help the youth grasp how to visualize sin and contrition. Sin is an abstract concept. It is easier to grasp with visuals that show our moving away or moving closer to the presence of God.

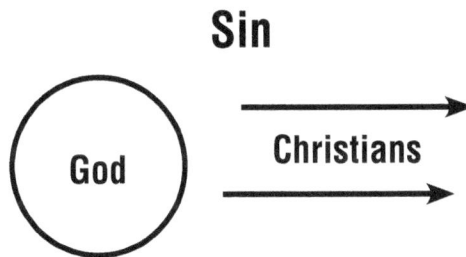

Sin

Sin is thoughts and actions that distance us from God.

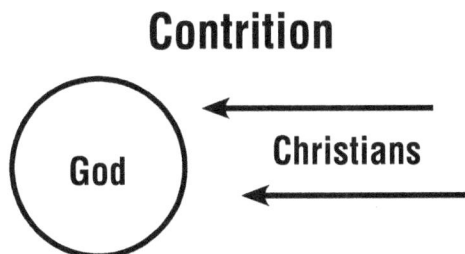

Contrition

Contrition is turning one's life around and seeking forgiveness to be closer to God's presence.

Sin is when we move away from God, and contrition is when we move back toward God. Moving back toward God is a lifelong process. Contrition (repentance and forgiveness) is finding ways to get closer to God again. Repentance is realizing that Jesus is to be a central part of our lives. This realization causes us to make new choices we would not have made had Jesus not become such an important part of our lives. Forgiveness is a primary way to heal all that is broken and not right with God and others. Contrition is a path that leads us back to God.

Our Relationship with God

Next, talk about the various aspects of our relationship with God, as described in the class outline in appendix B. Benefits include God's unending love, guidance, never being alone, eternal life, and instruction for daily life. Expectations include making God first in our lives; using our time, energy, and resources to serve God; loving what God loves rather than what we love; and being a part of a church community. Applications include prayer, reading the Bible, learning, worship, serving, and compassion.

It is important to be honest with God in how we live out our faith toward God and one another. Our prayer life with God should include asking for forgiveness, letting God know what we want to be forgiven for, asking with the right heart, letting God receive our asking, allowing God to remember our sins no more, and receiving God's grace.

Forgiveness Exercise

Share together an exercise in forgiveness. Have a bowl of water that is already in the middle of the table. Pass out a small stone or rock to each person in the class. Ask the youth to consider something they need to change in their lives: a relationship that needs to be healed, a way for them to grow closer to God, or how they might be better followers of Jesus. Tell them they will have a time of silence to think about one thing that want changed. When they have each thought of that one thing, they are invited to place their stones/rocks into the bowl of water. Tell them this action is like placing their requests to God in water that is renewing and cleansing and to make sure their hands feel the cool water. Also tell them they will not have to share their requests to God with anyone else in the room. Their requests are between each of them and God alone.

Scripture Discussion

Invite the group to open their Bibles to Luke 19:1–10. This is a story about a man who changes his way of life because of his encounter with

Jesus. The story of Zacchaeus shows people can change, just as Paul did. Our connection with Jesus helps make this possible. Jesus made it possible for Zacchaeus to find new meaning and inclusion with the community in which he lives. Without this new path and decision he would still have been considered an outsider or despised. His new decision to follow Jesus led him to more compassionate ways to relate to God and others.

Contrition Exercise Worksheet

Pass out the Contrition Exercise worksheet for the class members. Invite each youth to complete one and bring it to the next session.

Closing Prayer

Close the session with prayer. Teach the group to pray in silence. Ask them to listen to God in silence, pay attention to what enters their thoughts during the silence, and ask them to consider what God would say to them in a prayer of listening.

Supplies Needed

- Copies of the session outline to hand out at the beginning of your time together (see appendix B) or write the outline on a board or paper for all to see
- Pencils/pens and paper for the class members to take notes
- Bibles for all class members for the scripture discussion
- Chocolate chip cookies for the whole group
- A bowl of water and enough rocks for the forgiveness exercise
- Copies of Contrition Exercise worksheet to pass out at the close of the session

SESSION 5: Contrition
(experiential)

Open the session with prayer.

Tell the youth about the kind of experience they will have today. The goal of the session is to bring emotion and real life into the concepts of contrition (repentance and forgiveness). The critical part of this session is choosing the right venue to capture these elements in an experiential way.

It is important for them to hear a modern or current story of contrition that will mirror in some way what they learned about Paul and Zacchaeus in the Bible.

I have often chosen a ministry site that helps people and then invites them to improve their lives with faith rather than choosing a site that simply hands out goods to people in need.

Sample Experience Session: I chose a place near the homeless district of our town. The location uses a faith-based approach to helping people. Many of the homeless they service desire a second chance at life. The center has two functions: (1) it houses people and provides them meals, and (2) it serves meals to nonresident homeless at some meals. In both cases those who receive meals are invited to attend a worship service prior to the serving of food. I chose this place not only for the change they make in people's lives, but because of the fact they give former homeless people a chance to work at the center and give back to a place that has altered their lives in a significant way.

I took the youth to this location and had them experience two things. First, we walked through the facilities to view one of the sleeping rooms, the cafeteria, and the chapel. I then arranged for the group to hear the story of one of the workers who was formerly a homeless person. They were able to see firsthand a person who was changed by a place that communicated and lived the Christian message.

The main purpose of this experience was to encounter a face-to-face story of contrition.

The final part of the experience is to have the youth talk about their experience on returning to the church. Ask the youth what they saw, what they heard, and what they felt while at the location. Seek to draw out some of the emotional and spiritual aspects of the experience rather than the factual and obvious lessons of such a location.

Close the session with prayer.

SESSION 6: Covenant
(classroom)

Theme: Covenant

Class Concepts:

- Two visible ways we make covenants with God: using words and using symbols
- Baptism as a journey and a pilgrimage instead of an ending or destination
- Communion as a way for us to remember and honor Jesus by being faithful in the future
- Share how baptism and communion are a vital part of the church's worship life
- Teach that baptism is a one-time event, but communion is a repeatable event for Christians

Scripture Emphasis: Matthew 3:13–17 and Mark 14:22–25

Theological Foundation

- Baptism and communion are meeting grounds between God and us
- Baptism is the initiation of a covenant relationship that leads into eternity
- Communion is a constant reminder of the covenant we made through our baptism
- These sacraments or ordinances of the faith define and continually shape us as followers and disciples of Jesus Christ
- The covenant nature of baptism and communion is meant to be both individual and communal: *individual* transformation, and *communal* affirmation and support

Class Outline for Leader

Opening Prayer

What Is a Covenant?

It is important for youth to know about the *covenant* as it is used in the Bible and in the life of the church. It is not a common word for youth to use. They are more accustomed to words such as *contract* or *agreement*. Write the word *covenant* on a marker board or flip chart. Ask the youth if they know what the word *covenant* means. Leave some time for them to give their answers. A covenant is a mutual relationship in which two parties agree to be connected with intention and devotion. The Bible is filled with covenants that God makes with God's people to help people understand how much God loves us. The church celebrates two very important covenants through our worship service. The covenants are baptism and communion. They are visible ways for us to understand and grow in our spiritual life and in our connection to God's love of us. The focus for the day is helping the youth begin to grasp the value and power of covenants through the avenue of the two sacraments we practice in the Christian faith.

Discussion of Baptism Images

It is important for the youth to begin connecting the event of baptism with images that speak about aspects of faith and formalizing a relationship with Jesus Christ. Below is a list of images. Ask the youth what comes to mind or what they think those images mean in relationship to baptism.

Water	New Self
Death	Clean
Eternal Life	Community
Old Self	

After each of the youth share reflections on these images and words, speak about how baptism is a beginning place for a lifelong relationship with Jesus Christ. Those who choose to be baptized are embarking on a journey that is surrounded in God's love.

The "Highway" Model

A helpful way for the youth to understand the journey or pilgrimage concept of baptism is to think of the journey of baptism much like a highway.

You can draw the lines for a highway on a marker/chalk board and draw the following items on that highway to help them realize the ongoing journey they will share with others in the Christian community of faith.

1. Place drawings of cars on the highway (tell them these cars are like people following the Christian way who are already baptized)
2. Draw an on ramp to the highway and place a car on the ramp (this car is like them: ready to be baptized and join others already on the journey)
3. Draw a car that is stopped on the side of the highway that is broken down (this is a car that runs into trouble or struggle, just like us who have difficult moments in our lives and are slowed in our journey)
4. Draw different numbers on each of the cars. These numbers are equivalent to the number of years a person has been a Christian person. The point is that it does not matter how many years we are Christians, but rather that we join together in our common journey with Jesus Christ)

Visit the Baptistry

It is important for the youth to step inside the baptistry and see what it is all about. Revisit some of the image words used earlier in the session as you stand together in that location of the sanctuary. Those words will mean more to the youth once they are in the place they will be baptized. The visit as a class will help reduce anxiety they might feel about being baptized. Return to your classroom when finished in the baptistry.

Thinking about Communion

Shift focus to the understanding of communion. List the following terms on the board: remembrance, celebration, thanksgiving, Jesus as human, Jesus as divine, bread of life, and cup of salvation. Tell the youth that each of these terms helps us to better understand what is going on when we share in eating the bread and drinking from the cup during the communion time of the worship service. It is a time for individuals to be drawn closer to God and for the whole community to find strength as a church family in being with God.

New Testament Meal Pattern

Share some of the New Testament passages that have communion impact on the church's celebration of that act in worship. Three passages that help best to capture the meaning of communion are: (1) the feeding of the 5,000,

(2) Jesus' meal in the upper room with the disciples, and (3) the Emmaus story. Each of these involves a formula that is used in communion today. The formula is found in the sequence of verbs. In all three stories we find these same words: *took, blessed, broke,* and *gave.* These words become a way for Jesus to share important meals with the crowds, the disciples, and the faithful followers after the resurrection. The church today retains these words in the sharing of communion as part of our connection to those in the past, our current celebration of God's presence among us, and our passing on of these gifts to the next generation. They are words that give guidance on how we are to share this meal with our Christian brothers and sisters.

A Meal That Stretches across Time

It is important to share with the youth how communion has meaning for the past, present, and future. It is important for the youth to sense communion as more than a meal that happens in worship to remember Jesus. Communion binds us to God, connects us in spirit to those of the Christian faith throughout time, and is an experience that makes us whole through Jesus Christ. Below is a list of some of the past, present, and future elements of communion:

Past

Remember Jesus
Remember God's love for us
Remember our baptism

Present

Receive forgiveness from God
Reflect on how to live a life of faithfulness

Future

Great promised banquet
A time of new beginning and renewed sense of self

Connecting Baptism and Communion

Baptism and communion are considered sacraments or ordinances. The two moments in worship are unique ways in which we encounter God through symbols and experience. Both circumstances create closeness with God while surrounded by the wider community of faith. However, the youth should be taught a primary difference between baptism and communion:

- *Baptism is considered a nonrepeatable sacrament:* this is an event we celebrate once—we are baptized into the Christian family, and not a particular congregation or denomination. A person's decision to be baptized marks the formal beginning of a lifelong journey with God through Jesus Christ.
- *Communion is a repeatable sacrament:* this event in worship is about being reminded of our baptism and continuing a relationship with Jesus Christ. Communion provides the opportunity to find strength in God and find newness from the things we seek to leave behind or ask God to forgive.

Covenant Exercise Worksheet

The idea of baptism and communion being covenants is fundamental in creating a relationship of depth with God and Jesus Christ. Covenant implies our participation is more than casual or occasional. Covenant suggests we become fully engaged to seek, encounter, and follow God's leading. God never stops loving us. We, too, are invited to never stop our relationship with God. Baptism is our formal entrance into this covenant, and communion is our on-going act to remind us of this covenant relationship that is eternal. Baptism is *creating* covenant and communion is *renewing* covenant. Invite youth to examine the covenant of communion with the Covenant Exercise worksheet.

Closing Prayer

The closing prayer for the day is about thanksgiving and being grateful for what God has given us. Gather in a circle and have the group share one at a time two things they are grateful God has provided.

Supplies Needed

Copies of the session outline to hand out at the beginning of your time together (see appendix B) or write the outline on a board or paper for all to see

- Pencils/pens and paper for the class members to take notes
- Bibles for all class members for the scripture discussion
- Marker board or flip chart for use in class discussion and highway model description
- Covenant Exercise worksheet to pass out at the close of the session

*"Covenant suggests we become fully
engaged to seek, encounter,
and follow God's leading."*

SESSION 7: Covenant
(experiential)

Open the session with prayer.

Tell the youth about the kind of experience they will have today. The goal of the session is to bring the images of water, light, bread, and cup to life in a new way. The hope is to help youth have a better historical, theological, and emotional connection to how we form covenant with God through Jesus Christ.

The preparation for this experience session is very important. The intention is to create as much of an "upper room" environment for the youth as possible. Pick a room in the church that will be most suitable to host such decoration. This is to be an experience to heighten their aesthetics of the Lord's Supper. The goal is to engage the right side of the brain. You will be sharing a recreated upper room time with the group by talking about the background and significance of the meal shared with Jesus and the disciples. The time concludes with you washing the feet of the youth.

You can do the following with the preparation of the room to raise the level of engagement with the youth:

- Use a low table that you can gather around by sitting on pillows. Get the youth away from the traditional table and chairs arrangement. Bring the tables lower to the ground and cover them with nice table covers.
- Utilize natural light instead of electricity. Place numerous candles or oil lamps throughout the room to help set a reflective mood in the room. Try to prevent any light coming in from outside windows. Try to create the feeling of nighttime. Flames soften the mood and raise awareness that something special is happening.
- Make sure the room has a cross and Bible displayed prominently.
- Place the following symbols on the table the youth will sit around: light source (at least two or three candles), pottery plate with loaf of

bread, pottery cup with grape juice, wooden or pottery bowls with grapes and cheese in them, and a large pottery basin of water with a small hand towel that hangs over the edge. All of these items are important symbols of our faith, but each will be used as instructional tools in the upper room encounter.

- You might want to make use of a water element or music as a soft backdrop to your time in the room with the youth.
- Make sure the youth do not see the room before you lead them in for this experience. You want to let the entrance into the room heighten their raised awareness of a new experience and generate greater receptivity to your leadership in the encounter. Briefly explain to the youth that they will learn why the bread and cup are an important part of the Christian faith and of weekly worship.

Invite the youth into the room and ask them to find places to sit around the table. Ask them to do this in a quiet manner. Once everyone has found a place around the table you can begin the upper room experience.

Begin, "Today, we step back in time to the first century. We have entered a special room that was visited by Jesus and his disciples. They were in the city of Jerusalem, celebrating the Passover meal like other Jewish families and groups. They were in a room filled with light from candles or oil lamps. It was a quiet place for them to be together and share food, fellowship, and meaningful conversation with one another. It was in the midst of sharing that Passover meal when Jesus halted the meal and began speaking to the disciples about the significance of some of the elements found on the table in front of them."

"Jesus took bread, shared a blessing for the bread, broke the bread, and gave bread to each of the men in the room. He said, 'This is my body broken for you.' He then took the cup and said, 'This is a new covenant in my blood poured out for you for the forgiveness of sin.' Each took the wine as it was given to them."

"The disciples were definitely receiving a new teaching from Jesus about the bread and wine, but had no full comprehension he was speaking about his actual life that would be taken from him in hours and days to come. They had no idea that this 'broken body and spilled blood' was literally going to happen to Jesus. They probably thought it was another symbolic teaching about why Jesus had come to preach, teach, heal, and welcome people in God's name. They shared the elements of bread and cup feeling connected to Jesus, but not realizing this would be the final meal they would share with him before his death on the cross."

"As the meal continued, he stopped the disciples again. He stood up and removed an outer garment and took a basin of water and began to wash the feet of the disciples. The men tried to stop Jesus from doing so but failed. Washing the feet of a person was reserved for a servant or a person of little importance. This was no task for a man they believed was the Messiah. Despite the disciples trying to stop Jesus, he continued. He went to each man and took the water and washed his feet. It was an act of servanthood done in a spirit of love and compassion."

Invite the youth to remove their socks and shoes and turn their feet out away from the table so you may go by and wash their feet one person at a time. As you approach each youth, tell that person how much God loves him, how God believes in the gifts she has to make a difference in the world. Share this message with each person until everyone's feet are washed. Once this is done, continue with your talk.

"The night in the upper room would be a night those disciples would never forget. For one thing, it was a final meal with a man who had changed their lives. Another reason was that they made a special connection to Jesus and theother disciples, a connection that was different from other relationships they had in the past."

"The greatest power of this meal would not come until after the resurrection. When their friend Jesus was killed, it was a time of sadness. Their idea of who Jesus was did not come to pass. It was when the disciples gathered in an upper room following the resurrection that the meaning and significance of the bread and wine came to life for them. He had told them this bread and cup would be symbols of this sacrifice and love. He said they would be called upon to remember, and they now knew that remembrance was not only thinking about the past but about acting and making a difference in the future. The remembrance of that upper room meal with Jesus and knowing of his rising from the dead urged them from the upper room out into the world to spread the message of Jesus and God's unconditional love."

"The disciples entered God's kingdom on earth to proclaim the good news of Jesus. The fascinating and small detail that became an important part of telling Jesus' story was what the disciples found in every home they visited. If they were welcomed into a home to share company, they would find two items on every table. They would see bread and wine on the table. These were two common, everyday things a home would have that would be shared with guests. It was a natural connection between sharing fellowship around the table and sharing an intimate remembrance about a man that sought to change the world through love, sacrifice, humility, servanthood, and relationships. Jesus had provided the most powerful tool of evangelism to each disciple, and it already existed on every table of every home they visited."

"The disciples could remember. The disciples could proclaim. The disciples could talk about lives dramatically changed because of one man's ability to share openly and freely the love of God in the world. It just so happened that bread and cup became the primary symbols to share, experience, and live that story."

"Today, we entered a room that seemed dark at first, but the lights of this room gradually allowed us to see all that is important to our faith in Christ. We notice the Bible, which is our book of life and guidance for our Christian journey. We see the cross, which is the sign of Jesus' love that we might sacrifice for others to know of that love. We encountered the waters of renewal and humility, reminding us that no one is any more important than another person. We lastly encountered the bread and cup, which transform our lives to be all God hopes for us to be. We will leave this room filled with light so that we become the lights of the world to help others know of God's message of peace and hope."

Invite the youth to leave the created upper room and enter another room for the closing time together.

The final part of the experience is to have the youth talk about their experience. Ask the youth their impressions of the upper room encounter. You can ask them some of these questions:

- What did it feel like to be in a room made to look like the upper room Jesus was in with his disciples for the Last supper?
- What did it feel like to have your feet washed by your minister/ leader?
- Why is bread the kind of food used during communion?
- Why is grape juice or wine used during communion?
- What are we to remember when we eat the bread and drink from the cup?
- Who is the host of the meal?
- What will you tell other people if they ask you what communion means?
- What symbol in the room best helped you feel God's presence today?

Close the session with prayer.

*"Community in the church suggests we need
and lean on one another to embody what
Christ came to teach and demonstrate."*

SESSION 8: Community
(classroom)

Theme: Community

Class Concepts

- Creating community: (1) developing community within the church, and (2) developing community with those who are not a part of the church
- Community forms through intention and effort
- Community in the church is strengthened by the Holy Spirit
- Community is realizing that we can accomplish more together than we can alone

Scripture Emphasis: 1 Corinthians 12 and Luke 10:30–37

Theological Foundation

- The church is intended to be a communal experience celebrating God's presence rather than just a solo faith journey
- Christians are called to grow and learn from one another how to live and share the Christian life
- Jesus organized his efforts to share the kingdom of God with disciples instead of proclaiming that message alone
- God seeks us through a relationship with Jesus Christ, just like we discover the power of relationship in the church by celebrating Jesus Christ

Class Outline for Leader

Opening Prayer

Story of the Seed

Begin the session by talking about a seed. Hold a seed of any kind in your hand and tell the youth what this seed is capable of doing. Ask them if the seed can do all of what they say by itself. What does it take for a seed to develop into a plant or tree? Invite what is needed for the seed to grow and mature. Remind them that a seed cannot grow unless several factors are included. Sun, rain, and soil are the basics. Communicate that Jesus shared that even the smallest of seeds can produce a tree of significance, but it needs help. Today the focus will be on what it takes for the church to fulfill its mission and purpose. It achieves its mission and purpose by joining together in Christ's name. It is done together rather than alone.

Purpose of Community

Talk with the group about the purpose of community. Share with them some of the important elements of being together in community. Share with them they will learn about community in two ways: (1) the inner church community, and (2) the community/neighborhood surrounding the church. The first part of the session will be about the inner church community and the second half of the session will be about the community/neighborhood surrounding the church.

Inner Church Community

Community within the church provides an environment in which several components are happening at the same time. The church community has many functions. Some of these include: we need to be in Christian community because our growth in faith is discovered by learning from others in the church; we need to be in Christian community because we have the opportunity to aid others in their journey of faith; we need to be in Christian community to offer support and encouragement to others during times of struggle, need, illness, grief, celebration, joy, and discovery; we need to be in Christian community to accomplish more in the name of Christ together than we could ever do by ourselves; we need to be in Christian community because it is how Jesus taught us to live as people of faith. Community in the church suggests we need and lean on one another to embody what Christ came to teach and demonstrate.

Read together the full chapter of 1 Corinthians 12. The chapter shares two important truths about the church that are important for our understanding of the church today. The first truth is that we need one another because we have such a diversity of gifts. In the midst of our diversity, God calls us to find ways to share our gifts in a common cause to serve Jesus Christ. The second truth is that our oneness in Christ is about unity and not uniformity. We are not all to be alike. We are to embrace our differences to serve Christ, knowing our differences allow us to serve others because of the rich forms in which our faith is shared as a community.

Draw a rough picture of a body. Explain that each person in the church is like a different part of the body. What would happen if one of the body parts was missing? Missing that body part would limit our abilities. What if we were all the same body part? We would not be a body but rather all the same body part, with minimal function. The body is at its greatest potential when all the body parts are working and connected. The church is like the body in that we need everyone because everyone is unique and has a part to play in living out God's hope for the world. We rely on one another to share the love Christ gave to us.

Next, take out a ball of yarn. Ask the group to form a circle. Instruct the group that you would like to have each person answer the same question three times on three separate occasions. The question the youth are to answer is, "What activities do you like attending in the church?" The leader begins by answering what he or she likes to do in the church. The leader holds onto the end of the yarn and tosses the ball to one of the youth (*not* the person directly on either side of leader). That youth gives one answer to the question of what he or she likes to do in the church, holds onto the yarn, and then *gently* tosses the yarn to another person in the group (again, *not* the person on either side of the youth). Have this activity continue until everyone has answered the question three times. The group will notice that the yarn stretching from one person to another looks like a web.

The web is a visual to show how we are each connected to all the activities we like and participate in throughout the church. The church needs full community participation and activity to allow the web to be complete. Ask one of the youth to release his or her part of the web. When one person drops a portion, the web begins to break down and fall apart. The web shows how we need one another for the web to work. The same is true for our connection and involvement in the church. Share that the church is a combination of one large group and several small groups. The large group occurs when we gather for worship. The smaller groups are the different ministries, programs, and activities available for people to deepen their faith or serve others in Christ's name. Ask the group if they know the difference between the church community and other groups outside of the church. What makes the church different? Invite the youth to share and talk about what is unique about the church and following Jesus Christ.

Community outside the Church Building

The second half of the lesson involves talking and discussing how the church is related to the community outside the church walls.

Take a map of your city and lay it out on the table. Have the group gather around the table to look at the map. Draw a circle or make a mark to identify the church location on the map. Have the youth look at what is nearby the church. Is it mostly homes? Are there lots of businesses and restaurants? Are there parks or schools nearby? Have them think about what is close to the church.

Open the Bible to Luke 10:30–37 and read the story of the good Samaritan. As you complete the reading of the story, remind the youth that the story is about what being a neighbor is about. Who is your neighbor and how should you care for your neighbor? Ask the group who their neighbors are. Are your neighbors the people you live next to? People in your family? Friends and people you know? People in the church? Strangers on the street or in stores? Where do we draw the line for determining who is our neighbor? Did Jesus ever meet anyone that was not his neighbor?

- Who is our neighbor? is the key question when it comes to determining what community is outside the walls of the inner church community. It invites all kinds of questions about the church's involvement in the local community.
- Where does the boundary end for neighbor?
- Who is the church called to serve and reach out to?
- Why do we even worry about people outside the church?
- How well do you know all these neighbors?

Once we determine whom we will serve as church, the next decision is how best to serve our neighbor. There are a number of levels or ways for us to reach out to our local community (city, country, and world).

- *Giving money*—using our money to help people and agencies help others (the easiest form of reaching out)
- *Collecting items*—this is like having a food or clothing drive for people who need these items; it is a step up in personal investment from writing a check or giving cash to offer assistance
- *Volunteer our time to help others*—this form of reaching out has groups going outside the church and entering the experiences of others

where the need exists; this is where relationships and change happen both to the one served and the one doing the serving

- *Mission outing*—a group goes outside the church and travels for an extended trip to be in a place to serve people; the intent is to be more aware of how others live in difficult circumstance, and not quickly return to your comfortable homes; the elongated trip allows for more absorption of the needs and desperation people find themselves in around the world; a mission outing like this is an isolated experience
- *Adopting a cause for the long-term*—this form of mission and reaching out is similar to a mission outing except that members of the church make a longer term commitment to a place with time, resources, people, and money to make a sustainable impact for those being served
- *Being a part of changing laws and rules of caring for others*—this form of reaching out and serving others gets at the heart of community change; it is being proactive about lives being different by enacting laws to make people's lives better, rather than be reactive and trying to undo what is already broken

Discussion of Community Outing

The final conversation for this session involves determining what the experience session for community will be the next time. Tell the youth they have a decision to make. Let them know that they have one of two choices for a project the next week. No choice is wrong. They are to choose a project at the church to do to give back to the church community that supports them, or they can choose a project to make an impact in the local community around the church. Both ways of serving community are positive and both are needed. Let the group talk and decide how they want to proceed. Once their decision is made, you will tell them you will organize the project and let them know what will happen before they gather the next time, so that they can be ready to serve the community.

Closing Prayer

Supplies Needed

- Copies of the session outline to hand out at the beginning of your time together (see appendix B) or write the outline on a board or paper for all to see
- Pencils/pens and paper for the class members to take notes
- Bibles for all class members for the scripture discussion

- Marker board or flip chart for group discussions
- Seeds for the opening activity and for the class members to hold
- Ball of yarn for the sharing activity of church likes
- City map for community discussion
- Community Exercise worksheet to pass out at the close of the session

*"Community in the church suggests weneed
and lean on one another to embody what
Christ came to teach and demonstrate."*

SESSION 9: Community
(experiential)

The experience session for community will be in one of two categories. The youth will have made a decision in the previous session of which choice they want to make in sharing community with others. They either choose to do a project for the church or to do a project in the local community outside the church. The aim of the project is for them to understand how important it is to be in relationship with others. God seeks for us to be in community and in fellowship with one another. The community experience session is much like a service project for the youth.

If the youth decided to accomplish a project for their church, it is important to do a project that people in the church can see or hear about soon after it is completed. Below is a listing of a few examples of what the group could do for their church projects:

- It could be a planting/weeding project. The church grounds are always in need of care and maintenance. The group could adopt a flowerbed or sacred area on the grounds to improve/clean/upgrade in some way. This is a very tangible way for them to share their time, and it is relatively easy for others in the church to see the results of their work.
- If the group is musically gifted, they could come up with a song (sung or played) and practice that piece of music to share in worship during the coming weeks. The church would see the class sharing with the church and praising God at the same time. You could highlight the reason the group is sharing the gift of music on this day: it is a response to what they are learning about being faithful followers of Jesus Christ.
- The group could go over to the home of one of the members who is homebound and do some projects around that home that would

be helpful (yard care, house cleaning, visiting/storytelling, or other various needs in their home for minor repair or maintenance.)

• If the group is artistically talented, they can work on a banner or art piece that shows symbols or words highlighting the importance of community in the life of the church.

If the group decides to carry out a project in the local community, then you will find below a few examples of what can be done with the group's time on that day:

• The group can adopt a section of a street near the church and pick up all the litter in that area. It is much like the adopt-a-highway concept. It is a way to beautify the neighborhood near the church.

• The group could visit a nursing home, assisted care facility, or retirement center to sing songs, play games, or join in one the scheduled facility activities with the residents. Older individuals love to be around young people.

The purpose is to allow youth to experience how serving others in community can make a difference.

*"The words melt, mold, fill, and use describe
a process in which we allow God to
utilize our God-given potential."*

SESSION 10: Connection
(classroom)

Theme: Connection

Class Concepts

- Each person has gifts given by God
- Each youth is special and is created in God's image
- Individual gifts are combined with other people's gifts to serve a greater purpose
- They learn that once they determine their gifts, other gifts can develop in their Christian journey

Scripture Emphasis: Genesis 1:26–27 and Galatians 5:22–26

Theological Foundation

- God blesses us with spiritual gifts to share with others
- We are all created in God's image and reflect God to the world when we share these gifts
- The Holy Spirit is that presence Christ imparted to us to guide and strengthen us for the Christian journey and for sharing our spiritual gifts with others
- The discovery of spiritual gifts enables us to share our lives to benefit the mission and purpose of the church

Class Outline for Leader

Opening Prayer

You Are Special

Begin by reading a short book entitled *You Are Special* by Max Lucado. This book works well because it is relatively short and is a fun way to identify that each person God creates is important and valuable. This book helps communicate everyone's importance in the world, even when they do not feel important or have a purpose yet defined in their lives. At the end of the reading, invite group responses on the book. If you do not want to use this book, then find a short book or reading that highlights the unique gifts God gives to us.

Scripture Discussion

Invite everyone to open their Bibles to Genesis 1:26–27. Read these two verses out loud. Communicate that all humans are created in God's image. This is to say that a reflection of God is present in each one of us. The Bible is clear that this is true for both men and women. All people are gifted by God to share their gifts of time and energy. All should have the opportunity to lead and help grow the church. Ask the youth what they think it means that God made us each special. There never has been or ever will be another person just like Bill, or Beth, or Jeff, or Maria (or any appropriate names). They are each a unique part of God's creation. They all have something special to share in the world. When we share our gifts, we honor the God-giftedness that is in all of us.

Spiritual Gift Exercise

Give each person the Spiritual Gift Exercise from appendix C Give the youth some basic instruction on how to mark the answers to each of the questions. The exercise will not take too long. When they complete the questions, you can give them the sheets to record and score their answers. Give them some guidance so that they mark the tabulation page right. When they complete the tabulation, have them circle the three totals that are the highest. The totals correspond to the eight gifts listed at the bottom of the tabulation page.

Each youth will have identified three gifts out of eight possibilities. The gifts are broad enough to leave room for growth and discernment on each youth's part. Each gift has a brief explanation of what the gift means. Talk to the group about the gifts they identified as highest for them. Were they surprised by which gifts were the highest? Are the results what they already thought of themselves? Did they find out anything new about themselves?

Gifts we receive from God are special. We can spend a lifetime sharing them with others. The other wonderful part of gifts is that we obtain new gifts or gain knowledge of other gifts through time and experience. You could score high on certain gifts today, yet take this gift exercise again in a few years and have a different outcome with your gifts. The important thing to learn is share from the blessings God has given to you.

Scripture Discussion

The Bible talks about spiritual gifts in a number of places. Paul writes about gifts that come from the Holy Spirit. Paul communicates with the church in Galatia about qualities and gifts that are vital for a healthy faith and church. Read to the group Galatians 5:22–26. List the fruits of the Spirit on a marker board or flip chart. Ask the group where they see these gifts shared in the church and outside of the church by Christians. Below the listed gifts, list the responses of how those gifts are visible. This allows the youth to tie the abstract gifts to concrete actions they witness.

Other Ways to Identify Spiritual Gifts

Some people discover their spiritual gifts through an exercise such as this one. However, there are other ways to discover gifts God has given to us and the church:

- *Asking God through prayer*—be in conversation with God about how you can be helpful and faithful to others
- *Internal feeling/passion*—pay attention to what excites and gives you energy
- *What we see in ourselves*—be aware of what you notice about yourself
- *What others see in us*—listen to the reflections and comments of others about you
- *Trial and error*—some gifts are discovered by trying new things and discovering what you do well and enjoy doing with your time

Combining Our Spiritual Gifts

Say to the youth, "A few weeks ago we talked about the church as a body. We discussed how important it was for everyone to be included in order to be the community God wants us to be. I want those thoughts to be in our minds as we discuss gifts. If God gives us *each* spiritual gifts to share with others, imagine what these gifts could accomplish when combined with *every* person's gifts in the church. If we listed every person in the church and what gifts they had, how many gifts would our church be able to share? Part of our discovery of gifts is learning who God wants us to be. The other part of learning about our spiritual gifts is realizing what God wants the church to be."

Being Open to the Holy Spirit

Pass out hymnals to the group. Ask them to turn to the song "Spirit of the Living God" (*Chalice Hymnal*, no. 259). Read the words to this simple but powerful song. The words of this song invite us to consider how we are to be open to the Holy Spirit and how we are to be blessings for God to others. The words *melt, mold, fill,* and *use* describe a process in which we allow God to utilize our God-given potential. The song communicates that we must be open to God and that our openness leads to growth and discovery of our Christian identity.

Our Gifts in Action

The last part of this session involves discussing what the experience session will be for next time. The goal is to decide on an activity that uses the newly identified gifts of the group from the spiritual exercise taken earlier. The youth are to think about what gifts they have been given, combine them together, and brainstorm an activity or project to make use of those gifts. The leader can help guide the discussion, but it is important for the youth to finally decide on what will be done for the next session. This process is to make use of their newly identified gifts and begin creating a confidence in their ability to share assertively their faith and offer expression of that faith to others.

Closing Prayer

Remind students that discovering and using spiritual gifts is an ongoing process and that prayer is a key tool. Encourage students to pray during the week for themselves and one another. The closing prayer will be a silent prayer in which the youth thank God for the gifts given to them and how they will share them with others.

Supplies Needed

- Copies of the session outline to hand out at the beginning of your time together (see appendix B) or write the outline on a board or paper for all to see
- Pencils/pens and paper for the class members to take notes
- Bibles for all class members for the scripture discussion
- The Max Lucado book *You Are Special* or other resource
- Copies of the spiritual gift exercise and tabulation pages from appendix C
- Hymnals or copies of the lyrics to "Spirit of the Living God"

"The words melt, mold, fill, and use describe a process in which we allow God to utilize our God-given potential."

SESSION 11: Connection
(experiential)

This activity was planned at the close of the Connection classroom session. The leader's job is to make arrangements and cover any details to ensure this activity goes as smoothly as possible. You want to celebrate what the youth, as a group, decided to do with their spiritual gifts. They will feel as though this activity was a way for them to express what God has given them. This experience session promotes future leadership in these youth to plan and decide on ministry in the church.

Open the session with prayer.

It is important for the group to gather back at the church following whatever activity was accomplished or started. Invite the group to share what it was like to do that activity. Ask, "Did it feel good to share with others gifts God gave to each of you? How will this activity shared today encourage you to do similar activities in the future?"

Close the session with prayer.

SESSION 12: Church

Theme: Church

Class Concepts

- Basic nature and purpose of church life
- The particular denomination or church affiliation of which you are a part
- Despite the many expressions of the church, we are all one in Christ
- Even though we are part of a church, our primary role is to be followers and disciples of Jesus Christ as a collective whole

Scripture Emphasis: Acts 2:37–47

Theological Foundation

- The church is the expression of faithfulness that comes from receiving the Holy Spirit following Christ's resurrection
- The foundation of the church is not about it being an institution but rather a result of people's collective work to serve in Christ's name
- The church becomes the hands and feet of Christ in the world
- It is important for youth to know from which Christian tradition they are a part in living out church life as Christ's followers

Class Outline for Leader

Opening Prayer

Church Pictures

The opening activity is a discussion about pictures you will pass around to the group. Acquire several pictures of churches (local, other parts of the country, other places in the world). Invite them to look at all the different pictures. As they look at the different pictures, ask them what it is that makes a church. When we are driving around town and pass by church buildings, how do we know which church to attend? Lead them in a discussion time of the true character of the church. It is not the building. It is the Holy Spirit in connection with the people that helps create a church. Lead them to affirm that a church is what the people in that building embody: worship, prayer, study, fellowship, and service to others.

Scripture Discussion

Have the group open their Bibles to Acts 2:37–47. This passage is toward the close of the Pentecost story. The entire chapter talks about how the disciples helped facilitate a movement of people who believed in Jesus and God's kingdom. The selected verses they will read together are about those who were baptized and how they shared life together when gathering in God's name. They were about four primary tasks:

1. *apostles teaching*— learning from those who knew Jesus, the religious tradition of Jesus' heritage, and Jesus' teachings and parables
2. *fellowship*—being in the company of one another for support and strength
3. *breaking of bread*—worship of God and reclaiming Jesus' influence on their belief and new life as people of faith
4. *prayers*—spiritual formation between God and others in the community of faith; learning how to communicate as individuals and as a community toward God

The text goes on to describe how the group shared with one another to ensure that everyone received care and that needs were met. The final traits mentioned about those early believers describe them as people with glad and generous hearts. This does not mean we are always happy and generous, but it does help us know the spirit of what the church is about in our sharing of faith with one another. We are about bringing joy to others and sharing what we have so others can experience joy, too. The joy and generosity is a response to the love we receive from God.

Formation of the Church

Share the following about the church's formation in the second chapter of Acts. The church began after the resurrection and ascension of Jesus. It was formed, as Jesus had taught, with the receiving of the Holy Spirit. You can point out the Spirit's activity in the early part of chapter two. The church becomes the expression of God's love following Jesus' time with us on earth.

Roles of the Church

Next, give each youth a piece of paper and a pen or pencil. Ask the youth to list what they think are the five most important roles of the church. It is important for them to begin to compare what they read in the Bible with how their own church practices ministry and serves Christ. Give them a few minutes to complete their lists. Have each youth share his or her list and why those five items were chosen. There is no right or wrong answer. It is a helpful exercise for the youth to begin to see how they understand the church's purpose and mission.

Different Churches

Using a marker board or flip chart, invite the group to name different church denominations or kinds of churches they know. List as many on the board as the group can name. Once a representative number of the various denominations and churches are listed, ask them why we have so many different kinds of churches. Denominations or independent churches form from differences of opinion about how to interpret scripture passages or how to address important issues for the church. Sometimes the differences form from different styles of worship. Another reason for various churches is differences on issues of who is and is not saved.

Your Denomination

Ask the group if they know to which denomination or church affiliation their church is connected. I will use the Christian Church (Disciples of Christ) as an example. If you are part of another affiliation I invite you to insert your particular church beliefs and structure.

The Christian Church (Disciples of Christ) began in the early 1800s. Ask if anyone can tell the group what the denomination's basic beliefs are. Pass out to the group the "Who Is the Christian Church (Disciples of Christ)?" handout from appendix C. Review this sheet and each of the beliefs and why they are important to the church. It is organized by mission, beliefs, and values. That is a simple and structured way to summarize this church tradition based on its beliefs.

The Christian Church (Disciples of Christ) publishes an annual yearbook. Grab this book and show it to the group. Ask them to name a city to see if another church in the denomination is in that city. Encourage each youth to name a city and look it up. You may or may not find a church in that city. The purpose is to show that similar churches to theirs can be located all across the United States and Canada.

The next part in sharing about the Christian Church (Disciples of Christ) is showing how the church is organized in its basic structure. Share that the church expresses itself in three ways: local church, regional church, and general church.

- The *local church* is comparable to the church they attend— it is a local congregation
- *Regional church*—locate a map of the region that shows the boundary of the region; communicate how many churches are located in that geographical region; tell the youth that the regional church is formed in order to allow many churches to partner together in sharing ministry and faith
- *General church*—locate a map of the world and show that the denomination includes more than 3,700 churches in forty-six of the states and in Canada, plus many in countries around the world, such as Puerto Rico, Democratic Republic of Congo, and New Zealand, among many others. Share that the churches include churches worshiping in English, Spanish, French, Creole, Korean, Japanese, Vietnamese, Samoan, Chinese, Filipino, Chin, Mongolian, and even sign language. This information is to show the diversity of our church as well as the unity in the midst of our diversity.

The goal is for the 3,700 plus congregations to work together, share resources, and share our faith to make a difference in the world. Our goal is to accomplish more together in an organized way than we could if each local congregation worked independently.

Say to the youth, "As we look at our own denomination, we are called to remember that we can partner with churches from other traditions to accomplish even more in Christ's name. We are to have a global witness of our faith. Jesus shared with his disciples the following words at the end of Matthew's gospel, 'Go therefore and make disciples of all nations' (Mt. 28:19a). The church is called to serve people near our local church and around the world."

Purpose of the Church

Say, "The purpose of the church remains the purpose we discovered in the book of Acts earlier. Some of the ways we are called to be church in the world include:

- We are examples of Jesus to the world
- We show others what love really means

- We reach out to those in need
- We help people create a deeper relationship with God
- We are called to work together in unity to serve Christ

"The important thing to remember about all the churches we see and encounter in our lives is that, even though we may find differences, we can always find common ground in our love and discipleship of Jesus Christ. Jesus Christ is what can bring us together in being the church on earth. The practical way this is accomplished is through our words and deeds. All of us are representatives of the church and Jesus when we claim ourselves as Christians. Being a follower of Jesus asks of us to be responsible and to live the name of 'Christian' with honor. This is how we best share the church as we keep the doors open fors other to join."

Closing Prayer

Supplies Needed

- Copies of the session outline to hand out at the beginning of your time together (see appendix B) or write the outline on a board or paper for all to see
- Pencils/pens and paper for the class members to take notes
- Bibles for all class members for the scripture discussion
- Pictures of churches
- Copies of "Who Is the Christian Church (Disciples of Christ)? or similar document for your denomination
- Denominational yearbook to look up churches in different parts of the world
- Map of your church's geographic region to show the relationship your church has to other churches in your own denomination

Mentor Component

Relationships are a vital part of the training process for young people preparing for baptism. Mentors can make an impact in a young person's life through their personal time and attention that cannot be accomplished through the group class sessions. There are several reasons for the mentor relationship.

- Provides one-on-one time between the mentor and the class participant that cannot be duplicated in the class sessions
- Fosters an intergenerational relationship that is important for the young person
- Reinforces material covered in class to deepen the concepts taught and experienced in the class sessions
- Allows nurturing of the young person's faith through directed activities that go beyond the material covered in the class
- The young person witnesses firsthand leadership in worship and in the ministry life of the congregation
- The young person witnesses how faith is visible in the life of a Christian beyond the boundaries of church activities

Christians value people in their faith journey who took time and energy to share with them. We can all look back and name some people in the church who were invaluable in teaching us about the church, our faith, and letting us know we were of value to the church and the world. Even though a mentor has selected activities and roles to fulfill with a young person through the baptism preparation process, the time feels more natural than time spent in the classroom or with the other class members. A one-on-one relationship allows a young person to open up and be his or her true self as the relationship grows and time spent together increases. I am a firm believer that relationships based on faith are a true gift. The mentor and the young person benefit and grow because of the relationship they develop. The young person's desire to learn about baptism is the reason for the relationship, and Christ is the foundation of this one-on-one relationship in the church.

Imagine the long-term impact of mentor relationships that are formed in the church. Many church leaders will have the opportunity to aid the youth in their process leading to baptism so that those young people will grow to be faithful disciples of Christ's church and God's kingdom.

Before going any further, we offer a word of caution. The church must systemically guard against the use of mentoring to establish an inappropriate relationship between an adult and youth. The church must make this program safe for its children, screening out potential predators or abusers. Unfortunately, there is no fail-safe way to know who is an abuser. Therefore, the church must develop some guidelines for the mentoring process. For example, the church may call mentors and youth to always meet in a public place, asking parents to arrange for the transportation of the youth. It is true that taking such safety measures may hinder or limit meaningful mentor relationships, but the danger is too great and the damage done by sexual abuse too severe to risk enabling a predator. Remember, it is *impossible* for the church to ensure that a mentor is not a predator, so the mentor program must not include private one-on-one meetings, and parents should be encouraged to not allow such private meetings after the official program is over.

Selecting Mentors

The matching process of connecting adults to youth is vital to the mentor experience. It is important to establish a foundation of time and effort given by the mentor for the youth. You want each youth to have some input into picking the person he or she will spend time with over the program, yet you do not want a mentor that will fall short of what is expected during the program.

The selection process begins at the orientation session. Each youth is asked to write down on a piece of paper three people they would want as a mentor. Mention to the youth they are to select people they recognize as leaders and who they believe they can learn from about the church and about being Christians. It is strongly suggested that male youth select male mentors and female youth select female mentors. Let the youth know you will do the asking and let them know which adults they will be teamed up with for the entirety of the discipleship program.

The success of an excellent mentor program can hinge on the minister or key leader asking the mentors instead of the youth asking directly. A minister or key leader can help an adult discern if he or she can truly fulfill all that is being asked. If the adult truly feels unable to complete the mentor covenant, then it is easier to say no to the adult rather than the youth directly. Adults have a hard time saying no to a young person. If an adult who agrees to a mentor relationship when asked by a youth is really too busy, then the relationship will be less than what other youth might experience who have fully committed adults. Adults respond best when they see specifically what is expected of them. Show them the mentor sheet of expectations and the mentor rationale (found in appendix D) in order to give them an honest look at what they are being asked to do. Mention to adults what an honor it is that youth see them as leaders in the church and want to learn about the church directly from them.

Once adults agree to serve as mentors, it is important to send a letter thanking them for their willingness to serve the church and the youth they will mentor. They are embracing a vital role for youth when responding positively as mentors. (A sample letter is available in appendix D.) Sending notes of "thank you" at the end of the process—thanking them for their hard work, time, and effort with the youth who selected them—is encouraged.

When the mentor relationship works correctly, it becomes one of the most valued parts of the discipleship process. The young person learns valued lessons from the mentor. Youth develop a meaningful intergenerational relationship. Youth tend to gravitate to other youth before developing relationships with adults, which is healthy developmentally. Mentored youth gain insight into one person's life, faith, and understanding of Christianity in the church. It has been my experience that many mentor relationships that formally end at the conclusion of the program continue informally for years. In a previous church where I conducted this program, an adult and youth I know still maintain a special connection with one another eight years after that youth was baptized. One-on-one relationships strengthen the quality of a person's self-esteem and expression of self. Mentor relationships mirror the type of relationship Jesus lived with his disciples (although is is clear that the disciples were adults.)

The Mentor's Relationship to the Minister/Key Leader

The leader of the overall program should keep in touch with the mentors throughout the process. Occasional contact will assure a level of accountability and positive communication to ensure a meaningful experience for the youth. The minister should provide the overall schedule of the classes to the mentors so they can encourage and engage youth with the topics, themes, and experiences encountered. Communicate with mentors the goals of the overall program. Goals to assist in giving the mentors direction include: (1) help youth learn what it means to be a disciple of Jesus, (2) provide enough insight and education to help youth make a more thoughtful decision about their baptism, and (3) help youth understand that baptism is a beginning place in their journey of faith and not an ending place or destination. These goals will help guide the mentors in how best to assist youth with questions and discussions they share with one another.

Explaining Mentors to the Church

Congregational support of youth going through the discipleship process is indispensable. Utilize church communication (newsletters, e-mail, etc.) to inform the congregation which youth are participating in the program and which adults will be mentoring them. It is helpful for congregants to know why the youth are shadowing their adult mentors during worship and on Sunday mornings. It is my experience that a congregation is excited for young people discerning about baptism and making Jesus Christ central in their life. They want to offer words of encouragement or other ways of offering support. It might benefit the church to know other kinds of activities and functions the mentors have with each youth for the program.

A Personal Word about Mentors

As a youth I did not have any formal mentors when I was considering baptism. I was fortunate to be in a church that celebrated young people and their decision of seeking baptism. I do remember adults intentionally encouraging me to participate in church activities beyond youth functions for my age. I recall an adult who asked me to co-lead VBS crafts. This had a huge positive impact on my self-esteem and ability to share gifts God has given me.

Since I began aiding youth in their decision of baptism and journey of discipleship, I have intentionally formed mentor relationships for each youth. The results have been incredible. The intergenerational impact of the mentor relationship fostered youth to engage in other future church events beyond what was designated for their age group. The process led to some youth joining the adult choir, becoming regular worship leaders, serving on church ministries task forces and committees. We can never underestimate the value that an adult (beyond parents) can have on a young person in the church seeking to know more about Jesus Christ, the church, and living into God's kingdom on earth.

Retreat Component

Purpose of the Retreat

The retreat comes at the end of the process. The intent is to allow the youth to be together for an extended period of time for reflection on three forms of relationships: God, creation, and others. They begin early in the morning and continue into the late afternoon. Concentrated time together allows for greater learning than shorter periods of time spread out over multiple sessions.

The retreat design is intended to be a concentrated ending for the group. Retreats provide the opportunity to build on relationships already formed. The day creates a greater opportunity for youth to detach from their normal routines and activities for the day. Time at church is normally for a couple of hours. The retreat is longer and allows the concepts of faith to be present to them for a longer duration. They will be thinking about faith more intently and may invite a new awareness about themselves as Christian people.

The retreat includes a series of activities that begins with worship and sends them out into the community to strengthen how they practice and reflect on the Christian faith.

The design of the day is for them to have three experiences. The group will then process and share together about those experiences at the end of the day. They have already shared much time together by learning about confession, contrition, covenant, community, connection, and church. Each of the "c" sessions focused on the theme for the day. The retreat is a way to blend those themes together in theory and practice.

It is important that you clarify with the youth and their families the significance of their attendance at the retreat. Encourage a few parents to attend to help with travel and supervision. Send a schedule out ahead of time to let youth and parents know what they will do and when to return to the church to pick up their youth.

The retreat at the end of the process allows the developed relationships among the youth to be strengthened. There is something about being together all day, traveling in cars, and sharing similar experiences that helps us grow closer to one another and develop deeper bonds. The entire discipleship process is primarily about relationships. The essential relationship is about how they come to know Jesus Christ in a theological and personal way. That relationship expands into how they understand their relation to God, others in the church (local church, denomination, and other traditions), others outside the church, and God's creation. What better way than to blend all these relationships together over one day. The retreat is an immersion experience.

The end result is not to answer all their questions, but rather to pique their curiosity and interest at a deeper level about the Christian life. If they are going through a passage of discipleship, they need exposure to what the passage will include in their Christian journey. The retreat is not meant to accomplish all of this. The retreat is a way to begin their journey beyond what a classroom experience or single activity achieves. Retreats by their very nature invite reflection, discernment, growth, and depth. Imagine the possibilities for young people who experience this retreat with a Christian foundation and focus.

Discipleship Retreat Concept

Overview

- The aim of the day is to explore more fully the three types of relationships we encounter in our Christian lives—God, creation, and others.
- The hope is for us to see different ways God wants us to live and interact in the world.
- We are to see that all three forms of relationships are connected and overlap.

Human-to-God Relationship

- This part of our retreat is about worshiping God—God is to be central to the life of Christians and teach us how to connect our words with actions.
- The disciplines for the worship will be prayer, scripture, and silence.

Human-to-Creation Relationship

- This part of our retreat is about our connection and responsibility to the earth that is entrusted to us.

- How are Christians to take care of the earth? How do we know this is part of our responsibility?
- What are ways we celebrate creation?
- What are ways we care for creation?
- What is your favorite nature place to go to? Why?

Human-to-Human Relationship

- This part of our retreat is about our connection to others and our service to others in our midst.
- What does Jesus teach us about relationships?
- Why should we use our spiritual gifts to connect with other people?
- Why do we help others? Is there anything different about Christians helping others and those who are not Christian helping others?

Organizing and Conducting the Closing Retreat Day

The retreat day is organized in three parts: exploring God, creation, and humanity. Each part is a way to understand our relationship to each part of our faith story. All three components in the retreat day help bring to mind the varied ways we are called to be faithful in the world.

It is important to find a day during which you can spend most of the day with the youth, using parental help with transportation and snacks. The most logical day to have the retreat is Saturday because most places you visit are open that day as opposed to Sunday. You need several hours to complete all three parts of the retreat day.

The day begins once everyone has arrived at the church. Spend some time going over the plan for the day, including the order of events and places you will be visiting, and allow any of the youth to ask questions about the day or what will be happening.

Begin the retreat with prayer.

The first part of the retreat will be the "Human-to-God" relationship. Make sure the sanctuary is well lit and that the temperature is comfortable. Arrange for an oil lamp or candle to be lit on the communion table. Appendix E includes a worship exercise for the youth to use that is three pages long. Tell the youth this portion of the retreat will be done in the sanctuary. Invite them to sit in the sanctuary wherever they feel God's presence the strongest. The exercise is to be done in silence, but if they have a question about any part of the exercise once it has started, they can simply raise a hand so you can go to that person and quietly answer the question. Once they sit down, they can open the worship exercise and begin their time with God. They will need a pencil and something hard underneath the exercise form for ease of writing, and a Bible. Tell them to take their time and that there is no time limit in completing the exercise.

Once you determine that everyone has completed the exercise, gather the youth together in one place in the sanctuary. Invite them to share what it was like to worship God. You might ask some of the following questions about the exercise:

- When asked to find a place in the sanctuary, wherever you felt God's presence the strongest, why did you choose your particular location?
- What was it like to be in silence with God for an extended period of time?
- What will you take with you from this worship time?
- Why do you think it is important not only to listen but to act as Christians?

Remind the youth that worship is not only meant for Sunday morning. God invites us to other worship opportunities. It is important to find time in the week that is about being with God. Time with God builds up our faith and relationships with God. The more time we spend with God the more comfortable we are in our sharing with God. We open ourselves to a more honest relationship with God. Worship is not something we graduate from. Worship is a living and active part of what it means to be Christian.

The second part of the retreat will be the "Human-to-Creation" relationship. This portion of the retreat is for the youth to encounter a place for high exposure to different aspects of God's gifts of nature and animals.

You should now transition from the church worship experience and drive to whatever location you have designated for your creation stop in the retreat. This location can be one of many places in your city or community—such as nature center, botanical garden, walking trail, park (national or state), or a natural setting such as a river or forest. The intent is to decide on a location that is as natural as possible. Attempt to be in a place that is free of city noise (cars, trains, etc.). The focus should be on celebrating what God creates and shares with us.

Once you arrive at your nature location, gather the group together and let them explore where you have taken them. They must each have a buddy. You can also assign adults to be with each group that wanders together. As the youth explore, ask them to pick up items (one apiece) that they find particularly interesting. Let them explore and enjoy the space. Invite them to use their eyes to see all they can see. Tell them to pay attention to details. Have them listen to the sounds that are in that location (birds, wind, water, etc.). Communicate where you will be if they have questions about something they see or hear. If they want to show you something they see, have them come and get you and take you to what they find fascinating. This wandering period will be between 30 and 45 minutes, depending upon the group's interest and engagement in the activity.

Gather the group at the conclusion of their wandering time. Open your Bible and read the following passages: Genesis 1:1—2:3 and Psalm 8. Next read the words to the following creation hymn: "All Things Bright and Beautiful" (*Chalice Hymnal,* no. 61). Talk to the youth about the gift of creation and how each part of creation is unique and an important part of the world in which we live.

A key word to discuss in the Genesis passage is *dominion.* Ask the group what they think it means to have dominion in God's world. Ask them what they think God believes dominion in this world means. Share how we are to be partners in caring for what God has entrusted to us. We are to be mindful of caring for all of God's creation (nature and animals). We are to be responsible and accountable for the environment and to do what we can to make the world we live in safe for us today as well as for the generations to come. We are to make use of these resources to live, but we are not to abuse or take advantage of what God has blessed us with on this planet. We are the one part of creation that has a mind and, therefore, knowledge to know when we are not caring for what God has given to us. We are not only the ones to whom God entrusts the world, but we are caretakers appointed by God. We must realize how each part of creation is connected to one another.

Read Psalm 8 to show the splendor and joy with which we celebrate all of God's creation. Remind the group how remarkable a place we live in every day. There is so much beauty around us if we open ourselves to see, hear, smell, touch, taste, and experience God's world. The joy of God's creation should shift to the joy of our sharing in its care.

Provide some time for the youth each to share the object of creation he or she was asked to select during the wandering. Ask the youth why they chose what they did. Invite them to share what was most meaningful to them in this time with nature.

The third and final part of the retreat will be the "Human-to-Human" relationship. Take the group from the nature location to the final stop in the retreat. This final destination is about how we as Christians relate to others in the world. Select a place that will allow the group to be of service to others and at the same time be representatives of the church in fulfilling that time of service. This activity can be done in a variety of ways. You will find below a small listing of examples of how to encounter the "human-to-human" component of the day:

- Serve a meal to the homeless at a soup kitchen
- Visit and play games with people in a retirement community
- Go to a homeless shelter, make meals for them, and visit with some of the residents of that shelter
- Go door-to-door asking for food to give to the local food bank, identifying yourselves as youth from your church.

The goal is to engage youth in an activity of compassion and caring for those who would benefit from Christian hospitality. Drive to the location you have decided upon. Talk to the youth before you leave the car and enter the place you are visiting. Remind them they are to show love through their actions and their words. Tell them that they can be examples of the Christian faith to each person they encounter and meet. Encourage them to visit and talk with as many people as they feel comfortable doing so in a safe way. Remind the adults who are helping with transportation to assist when they see the need. The purpose is to interact and help others with our time and gifts.

When the activity is over, the group is to return to the church. The final part of the retreat is talking as a group about the three activities of the day: worship time, nature location time, and service time. Allow the youth to share what they learned, what was new for them, how they demonstrated or shared their faith with God or others.

Communicate with the group the importance of balance in the Christian life. As followers of Jesus, we are invited to be mindful of how we live in the world God made for us. A primary part of our life is worshiping and praising God. We are to engage God in prayer, in song, in scripture, in silence, and in community. Another important part of our life is being good stewards of our world. Finally, we are to reach out to others just as Jesus continually reached out to others who needed God's love. For Jesus, this was everyone he met and encountered. We are to be examples and storytellers of Jesus' desire for all to know of God's unconditional love through paths of peace, wholeness, and compassion.

Close the retreat with a group prayer that allows each person to lift up something to God that touched his or her life that day.

The Role of Worship

Connecting the Youth's Preparation Process to Worship

Worship is the largest gathering of the church during the week. It is a time to praise God and celebrate lives being changed in Christ's name. The youth's exposure in worship should be continual throughout the time they are attending sessions and discerning about their decision of baptism. Each youth needs the support of the congregation. The congregation should be invited to pray and encourage each of the youth who decide to enter this learning time, journey of faith, and pilgrimage of baptism.

Introducing the Youth and Mentors

The minister or leader should introduce each youth and his or her mentor the Sunday following the agreement of those relationships. Each youth and mentor should be invited and encouraged to come so the congregation can see all the youth paired with their mentors for the coming months. The formal introduction of these relationships in worship will highlight their presence and participation in worship services throughout the process. It should be noted that the youth will be shadowing their mentors in whatever leadership role or function they might have during worship. Communicate it is a time for the youth to learn more about worship and the leading of worship. Select a time in the worship service that seems most appropriate to introduce these people. Every congregation handles these kinds of things differently.

The Shadowing of Mentors in Worship

Each week youth will be seeking out their mentors before worship begins. Each youth should know in advance if his or her mentor has a leadership role in worship that day. If the mentor has no role in worship, the mentor and youth will sit together in worship. The pair can sit next to the youth's family if they wish. This is not required. If the mentor does have a role in worship, then the youth will follow and aid the mentor if this has already been coordinated.

For example, if the mentor is an elder praying at the communion table, then the youth would stand beside the elder at the table during the communion time. The same would be true if the mentor was a deacon, part of the choir, worship leader, instrumentalist, etc. The concept is for the youth to begin understanding the leadership dimension of worship from a hands-on experience. This kind of experience is good for the youth to learn. It is also good modeling of leadership. Finally, it allows the congregation to witness a positive model of nurturing young people in the church. The congregation now sees the youth who is attending classes.

The shadowing process continues each week until the class sessions and baptisms are completed.

Confessions of Faith

If youth attending the classes decide it is the right time for them to be baptized, then they are asked to make a confession of faith. This confession of faith is best done in the worship service. It is an opportunity for the church to witness the young people's declaration about their faith and desire for Jesus Christ to be a central part of their lives. Most congregations have a time or opportunity for people to witness to their faith, join the church, or confess their faith in Christ.

If youth make this choice, welcome them on behalf of the congregation and celebrate this important decision in their lives. Invite the congregation to greet and celebrate with this person or persons and their families following worship. This gives opportunity for the congregation to give personal support and love to those making the next step in their Christian journey of discipleship.

When to Baptize?

This question may sound silly. Any Sunday is a wonderful day for a baptism. If you are embarking on this process for young people, it is important to plan the start of the program as well as the end of the program. The overall process is about twelve to fourteen weeks in length. You want to be intentional of when you want the program to end at an appropriate time in your church's calendar.

Many churches celebrate baptisms of youth at Easter. They are logically connecting the resurrection of Jesus with the resurrection or new life of a person who is baptized. It is a Sunday in which extended families are present to witness the baptism. It is also a time for visitors and guests to witness a sacred act such as baptism.

I want to make a theological and practical argument for youth baptisms to be celebrated on Pentecost. Easter is the great day of resurrection. The focus is on the empty tomb, the risen Lord, and the gift of new and eternal life received because of this glorious resurrection. Easter is a day for the church to celebrate who Jesus was, is, and continues to be for the church. If baptisms are celebrated on Easter they become one of many special moments in the service. Easter services are filled with baptisms, special music and anthems, and other traditions churches form on that day. I believe baptisms are much too important for the church for them to become one of many celebrations of the day.

Pentecost, on the other hand, is a day in the church's life in which we celebrate the formation of the church, the gift of the Holy Spirit, and the thousands of people who were baptized and sought to be faithful followers of Jesus. Isn't this what our baptism is about? Baptisms are a response to the resurrection and the gift of the Holy Spirit. The celebration of baptisms theologically connects well to the celebration of Pentecost. Finally, I think the church should talk more about baptism. We take few opportunities in the church to help us remember, reflect, reclaim, and continually live into our baptism. Pentecost provides an open doorway to that rich theological part of our church's story.

There are several reasons baptisms on Pentecost make practical sense. Since baptisms occurred on Pentecost in the Bible, it gives us, as a church, visible baptisms to celebrate on that day. The focus of the worship is on baptism for the church and the youth being baptized. The youth are no longer a small part of the service. They become an integral part of the worship's story and message for that day. Much of the worship's liturgy should and can include baptismal imagery and language. It is a day in which the church family can celebrate these young people with full attention and excitement. I made the shift of baptisms from Easter to Pentecost in three congregations. When I explained the theological and practical rationale to them, it was welcomed with little or no disagreement. So, for example, if the ending of the process is Pentecost, then the beginning of the process should be the middle of January to accomplish all the sessions.

Worship on the Day of Baptisms

Pentecost, with the addition of baptisms, is now one of my favorite worship services of the year. The Holy Spirit is often the hardest theological part of the faith to grasp and communicate. The celebration of baptisms gives a tangible and visible sign of the Holy Spirit at work in people. I love to plan, coordinate, and worship the Pentecost service.

I have included a sample order of worship in Appendix F for you to assess. You will notice in that order of service several things: the intentional weaving of the biblical story of Pentecost with the celebration of baptisms and how they naturally work together. This is true for scripture, music, prayers, sermon, and time following communion, which includes a special liturgy for the youth after partaking of communion. Included in that order of worship is a special confirmation covenant insert in which the minister, baptismal candidates, church spiritual leaders, and congregation share together. It is a wonderful way to celebrate the gift of newly baptized followers of Jesus Christ.

The power of the Holy Spirit is at work when you weave together music, prayers, message, baptismal water, bread, and cup. Pentecost Sunday can become a day that incorporates symbol, language, and experience to claim baptisms and celebrate the gift of the Holy Spirit in the church of Jesus Christ.

Appendix A: Orientation Handouts

Discipleship Class Orientation

1. Opening Prayer

2. Scripture Reading
   - Mark 1:16–18
   - Learning to be a disciple

3. Overall class content
   - Focus scripture for each area of learning
   - Session Themes
     Confession—learning what we believe
     Contrition—making Jesus the focus of our lives
     Covenant—a look at baptism and communion
     Community—internal and external expressions of our faith
     Connection—learning and sharing our spiritual gifts
     Church—our connection to other Christians
   - How our faith makes a difference in our daily lives
   - Learning to pray

4. Learning to live as a covenant people
   - Us responding to God
   - God responding to us

5. Mentorship
   - Choosing a person you admire to be a guide to do activities and learn from while at the same time learning in class sessions (make a list of three people and choose one of them)
   - Giving one-on-one time with a person to grow in relationship to him or her and learn about the life of the church

6. Class process
   - Each topic will have a classroom session and an experiential session
   - The classroom sessions will be a discussion as a group about the topic of learning and will include an assignment to complete by the next session
   - The experiential sessions will be us going out into the community and putting those classroom sessions into practice
   - The overall program will end with an extended time together: a day retreat

7. Questions

8. When to meet

9. Closing prayer

Discipleship Class Overview

Class Component

Session 1   Orientation with Youth and Parents
Session 2   Confession (classroom)
Session 3   Confession (experience)
Session 4   Contrition (classroom)
Session 5   Contrition (experience)
Session 6   Covenant (classroom)
Session 7   Covenant (experience)
Session 8   Community (classroom)
Session 9   Community (experience)
Session 10 Connection (classroom)
Session 11 Connection (experience)
Session 12 Church

Mentor Component

- Each youth is connected with a mentor for the duration of the class sessions
- The mentor and youth have continual things and one-time projects to accomplish together
- The mentor will provide insights about his or her journey of faith and connection to the church not covered in the class sessions and relate those insights to the subject he or she is leading in the sessions above

Day Retreat Component

The day retreat has three components
- Human-to-God relationship—prayer/worship experience
- Human-to-creation relationship—go to a creation setting
- Human-to-human relationship—care project for others

The purpose is to understand the three primary ways we relate in the world

The retreat is intended to come at the end of the twelve class sessions

Appendix B: Class Outlines

Confession Outline

Opening Prayer

Sentence Completion Exercise
- My name is…
- I was born…
- Three words that describe me are…
- Something important to me is…
- I am involved in the church because…
- I am in this class because…

Bragging Exercise

What Is Confession?

Scripture Discussion on Matthew 16:13–20

Other Christians' Confessions
- Disciples Affirmation (*Chalice Hymnal,* no. 355)
- Nicene Affirmation of Faith (*Chalice Hymnal,* no. 358)
- Apostolic Affirmation of Faith (*Chalice Hymnal,* no. 359)
- United Church of Christ Statement of Faith (*Chalice Hymnal,* no. 361)

First Person Exercise: Role-playing God, Jesus, the Church

Confession Exercise Worksheet

Closing Prayer

Contrition Outline

Opening Prayer

Chocolate Chip Cookie Exercise

Scripture discussion on Acts 9:1–19

What Is Sin?

Our Relationship with God
1. Benefits
    a. God's unending love
    b. Guidance
    c. Never being alone
    d. Eternal life
    e. Instruction for daily life

2 Expectations
    a. Making God first in our lives
    b. Our time, energy, and resources to serve God
    c. Loving what God loves
    d. Being a part of a church community

3. Applications
    a. Prayer
    b. Reading the Bible/learning
    c. Worship
    d. Serving
    e. Compassion

Forgiveness Exercise

Scripture Discussion on Luke 19:1–10

Contrition Exercise Worksheet

Closing Prayer

Covenant Outline

Opening Prayer

What Is a Covenant?

Discussion of Baptism Images

The Highway Model

Visit the Baptistry

Thinking about Communion

New Testament Meal pattern—"took, blessed, broke, and gave"

Meal That Stretches across Time

Connecting Baptism and Communion

Covenant Exercise Worksheet

Closing Prayer

Community Outline

Opening Prayer

The Story of the Seed

Purpose of Community

Inner Church Community

Scripture Discussion on 1 Corinthians 12
- Image of the Church as a Body
- Yarn Exercise

Community outside the Church Building
- City Map Exercise
- Scripture Discussion on Luke 10:30–37
- Who Is Our Neighbor?
- Ways of Serving the Community

Discussion of Community Outing

Community Exercise Worksheet

Closing Prayer

Connection Outline

Opening Prayer

You Are Special

Scripture Discussion on Genesis 1:26–27

Spiritual Gift Exercise

Scripture Discussion on Galatians 5:22–26

Other Ways to Discover Spiritual Gifts

Combining Our Spiritual Gifts

Being Open to the Holy Spirit

Our Spiritual Gifts in Action

Closing Prayer

Church Outline

Opening Prayer

Church Pictures

Scripture Discussion on Acts 2:37–47

Formation of the Church

Roles of the Church

Different Churches

Your Own Denomination

Purpose of the Church
- We are the examples of Jesus to the world
- We are the ones to show others what love really means
- We are the ones to reach out to those in need
- We are the ones to create a deeper relationship with God
- We are called to work together in unity to serve Christ

Closing Prayer

Appendix C: Class Exercises/Handouts

CONFESSION EXERCISE

Foundations of Faith

God—

Jesus Christ —

Church —

▪ ▪ ▪ ▪ ▪ ▪ CONTRITION EXERCISE ▪ ▪ ▪ ▪ ▪ ▪

How Do I Love?

A life of contrition involves learning how we are called to love God and what is in the world. List below some ways that you believe we are called to love God with our very best.

List below some ways that you believe God calls us to love other people: family, church members, friends, and strangers.

List below some ways that you believe God invites us to love ourselves.

▪ ▪

COVENANT EXERCISE

A Family Memory

I want you to put a picture in your mind of all your family members and extended family. Think of a meal in which all of you, or as many as possible, gather during the year. It is Christmas, Thanksgiving, family reunion, or other special time of the year. Try to recall as much as you can about your latest get-together on that occasion.

What makes this meal and get-together special?

What do you remember most about the meal and time together?

The church has a meal that is considered very special to its members and guests. That meal is our weekly time of communion. We break bread, share the cup, and are invited by Jesus Christ to share in that meal. It is a time to grow close to God, to recall how Jesus said this meal would call us to remember and celebrate. It is also a time to grow close to others who share the meal in that worship service.

Ask your parents why communion is important to them and write down some of their responses.

The Language of Our Church Music

Look up in the church hymnal the following songs: "When You Do This, Remember Me," "In Remembrance of Me," "Come, Share the Lord," and "I Come with Joy." Read the words of the songs.

As you read the words of the song, pay attention to the use of the following words: *remember, bread, cup, wine, forgiveness, free, family, joy, Jesus, share.*

If communion is able to help us experience all these words, then why do you think so many people see this as one of the most important parts of our worship experience?

⌐⌐⌐⌐⌐ YOUTH MENTOR HANDOUT ⌐⌐⌐⌐⌐

Interviewing Your Mentor about Baptism

Find a time to sit down with your mentor and have him or her answer the following questions about his or her personal baptism experience and what that baptism means to the mentor now.

1. What do you remember about the day you were baptized? How old were you? What church were you attending? What family was present?

2. Did you have any preparation or classes to help you better understand what baptism means? If so, what do you recall about that preparation process?

3. What was the most meaningful thing about your baptism?

4. Why did you feel it was important to be baptized at that point in your life?

5. When you are asked to remember your baptism, what comes to your mind?

6. Why do you think baptism is important for people who believe in Jesus Christ?

7. What significance does your baptism have for you today?

COMMUNITY EXERCISE

The exercise for community is to put together a puzzle of at least 100 pieces. Assemble the puzzle by yourself or with the help of your family. When you complete the puzzle, talk to your parent(s) about the following questions:

- What allows the puzzle to hold together?
- If you were missing one piece to the puzzle, would it be complete?
- How is the church like a puzzle?
- What happens if a person is missing from the church, like when a piece of the puzzle is missing?

The puzzle is an excellent example of how the church functions. The church is not about individuals gathering in the same place. The church is when we connect ourselves together to become the image of God to each other and the world. Everyone is needed to make this image. No one piece of the puzzle is more important than another. It takes all the pieces to create the image you are trying to see.

Share a prayer with your family for the blessing of all the people in the church and what they bring to the church to help it be a place of faith.

CONNECTION: SPIRITUAL GIFT EXERCISE

Discover Your Spiritual Gifts

Instructions

For each question, enter the number that most applies to you.

3—That's me! 2—This is probably me. 1—Definitely not me!

___ 1. I try to think more about the needs of others than my own.

___ 2. People come to me when they need to talk out a problem.

___ 3. I have given money to those in need.

___ 4. I don't mind being seen with people who aren't that popular.

___ 5. When I see needy people on cold nights, I really feel like inviting them to my home.

___ 6. On Friday nights, I am usually the one who decides where we go and what we do.

___ 7. I like to invite my friends to church.

___ 8. I have confidence that God will get me through both good and bad times.

___ 9. I like doing jobs that most people don't want to do.

___ 10. I am known for my positive attitude.

___ 11. I get a real kick out of giving stuff away.

___ 12. I would like to work with disabled people.

___ 13. I like having friends stay overnight at my house.

___ 14. I like to organize and motivate groups of people.

___ 15. I can sometimes make discussions relate to God.

___ 16. I believe that God can do things that seem impossible.

___ 17. I have helped other people so their work was easier.

___ 18. I like to help sad people feel better.

___ 19. I try to be smart with my money so that I can give extra money to people who need it.

___ 20. I feel very sympathetic toward the needy.

___ 21. I like having guests at my house.

___ 22. I have encouraged others to get better grades.

___ 23. I would like to help someone else become a Christian.

___ 24. I have confidence that God keeps promises even when things are bad.

___ 25. I don't mind doing little jobs that other people don't consider important.

___ 26. I can encourage others through what I say.

___ 27. I know that God will meet my needs, so I want to give freely to others.

___ 28. If a friend is sick, I call to see how he or she is doing.

___ 29. I like having company come to my house.

___ 30. I would like to help people who are homeless.

___ 31. I would like to tell others that Jesus is the Savior and help them see the positive results.

___ 32. I trust that I can call on God and know God will be there when "impossible" situations happen.

___ 33. Sometimes I do jobs and nobody notices, but I don't mind.

___ 34. I like it when people are happier after I have talked to them.

___ 35. I have given away my money or belongings to those in need.

___ 36. When I see a homeless person, I really want to help.

___ 37. My friends come over to my house because they feel comfortable there.

___ 38. When I'm in a group, sometimes people look to me to take charge.

___ 39. I take any opportunity I can to tell people about Christ.

___ 40. When everything looks bad, I can still trust God.

Discover Your Spiritual Gifts Tabulation Sheet

Instructions

1. Put your response (1–3) to each question in the blank next to the appropriate number on the chart below.
2. Add up the numbers going across the blanks and record them in the box under the "Total" column.

Test Question #	Your Response	Test Question #	Your Response	Test Question #	Your Response	Test Question #	Your Response	Test Question #	Your Response	TOTAL	GIFT
1		9		17		25		33			A
2		10		18		26		34			B
3		11		19		27		35			C
4		12		20		28		36			D
5		13		21		29		37			E
6		14		22		30		38			F
7		15		23		31		39			G
8		16		24		32		40			H

Explanation

Gift A—Helping: The ability to assist and serve other people.

Gift B—Encouraging: The ability to support people and help them to regain hope.

Gift C—Giving: The ability to give your time and money so it can be used for God's work.

Gift D—Mercy: The ability to act compassionately toward those who are suffering.

Gift E—Hospitality: The ability to be friendly and generous to guests.

Gift F—Leading: The ability to motivate others to use their spiritual gifts and to do their best for the work of the Lord.

Gift G—Evangelism: The ability to help others to come to know Jesus personally.

Gift H—Faith: The ability to have a confident belief that God will always do what is best.

Assessment

Determine your demonstrated, probable spiritual gift(s) as follows:
If the score in the "Total" section is:

10–15: There is great evidence that God has blessed you with this gift.

7–10: There is a good possibility that God could be developing this gift in you.

3–6: You are spiritually gifted in areas other than this one.

CHURCH

Who Is the Christian Church (Disciples of Christ)?

Mission

Our calling to the world is to go and make disciples of all people

Core Beliefs

- We confess Jesus Christ as Lord and Savior of the world
- We believe the unity of the church is essential to God's mission to the world
- We believe the primary authority for the church's life is the Bible
- We believe the Bible is the primary source of God's revelation Jesus Christ
- We believe in the empowerment of all people through the Holy Spirit

Values

We look to the church, God's community of love:

1. As a people of God
2. As the body of Christ
3. As a church both local and universal
4. As a community of faith inclusive, diverse, and welcoming
5. As a body that studies together and supports one another
6. As a body that worships celebrating baptism by immersion and observes the Lord's supper weekly
7. As a body that is in covenant with the different manifestations of the Christian Church (Disciples of Christ) – General, Regional, and Local

The communion table is our meeting ground at which we discover

1. Our commonness in Christ
2. The celebration of our diversity
3. A place to find an experiential connection to Christ
4. Our individual and communal voice as a church

Dialogue and discussion of theological topics is done in love and discernment to:

1. Hear each other's reflections and thoughts in a spirit of openness

2. Respect one another without being judgmental
3. Be open to a belief that might strengthen our faith
4. Have a healthier way to be in faithful conversation with one another
5. Model to those outside the church how to work through topics of importance, controversy, or crisis

Appendix D: Mentor Materials

Mentor Expectations Sheet

The mentor is to have contact with the youth throughout the duration of the program. Some of the activities done together are ongoing while other activities are one-time events. Below is a listing of things mentors are asked to do with their youth.

Ongoing Activities

- Weekly sitting with your youth in worship (he or she will be your shadow wherever you go, i.e., choir, elder, deacon, worship leader, etc.)
- Take your youth out to eat at least twice
- Call your youth on the phone to check in with him or her from time to time

One-time Activities

- Attend a church meeting with your youth
- Be interviewed by your youth about your faith and your reflections of your own baptismal experience
- Go over a worship bulletin to ensure your youth understands all the parts and, thus, the flow of worship
- Go over a church budget with your youth to help him or her understand the financial side of the church
- Take your youth to your place of work or where you volunteer to let him or her see you in your own environment
- Discuss and decide on a servant activity the two of you can do together

Education Objectives

- Informally talk about the main topics of learning done through the instructional and experiential classes
- Draw from the youth what he or she is learning
- Reinforce the point that he or she is on a journey and the end of the class is a beginning place for a richer relationship with God

- Help your youth understand that our faith in Christ is not only about knowledge of the Bible and God, but putting into action what it is we believe

The *minister* asks the mentors to serve, in order to make sure there is a firm commitment by the adult to work with the youth.

If the youth ends up being baptized, then the mentor is encouraged to give him or her a gift of celebration for that decision and special event in his or her life.

Mentor Assignment Rationale

The activities to be completed by the mentor and his or her youth are a vital part of the preparation of discipleship. Each request has a specific rationale that assists the young person in faith development, discovery of the church, and forming a closer relationship with the mentor. Below is the rationale behind each activity to give greater perspective, allowing a richer experience as a mentor.

On-going Activities

1. Weekly sharing with your youth in worship (he or she will be your shadow wherever you go, i.e., choir, elder, deacon, worship leader, etc.)

We sometimes learn more by what we do than by what we say. A young person can learn a great deal by observing another person in worship. Shadowing a person who takes part in the leadership of worship gives youth a different perspective of worship. At times he or she will be in front of the congregation without needing to speak. The youth gain a new appreciation for what a person does to prepare, lead, and participate in worship to praise God. The weekly, shared experience gives the mentor and mentored a way to engage and talk about worship, leadership, and faith development on a personal level instead of in a more formal teaching relationship. This process is also good in helping prepare young people to be comfortable in front of others as future servants in worship.

2. Weekly phone calls to the youth being mentored

It is important to keep the relationship between the mentors and mentored consistently engaged. The regular calls allow the youth to feel cared for and important when receiving calls at home. This is where the mentor relationship begins to form beyond the boundary of the church facility. It is important for youth to see how the congregation cares for and develops relationships away from the church building. Youth need to witness faith being applied in the daily life of church members.

3. Sharing meals with the youth being mentored (at least two times)

Sharing time around a table creates an informal time with the mentor and mentored. Shared meals feel less like an assigned task. The meal experiences are primarily meant to strengthen the relationship with informal time together. There is no agenda meant for the meals others than being together. It is only natural that the youth will learn and grow by the conversations shared.

One-Time Activities

1. Attend a Church Meeting

It is important for the youth to attend a meeting of any kind to observe how the church works in its dreaming, planning, organizing, and implementing time. Youth need to learn that the church requires dedicated people giving of their time and talents to create meaningful events for people to connect to God and Jesus Christ. The meetings attended may not be the most exciting events for the youth, but they will gain a new appreciation for how the church operates to serve others who engage in church ministry.

2. Be Interviewed by the Mentored Youth

Youth need to learn the story of others who are baptized and what they remember about their baptism. Each youth will be given a list of questions to ask the mentor. The questions will be about what the mentor recalls about his or her baptism, how important that event was in the mentor's Christian faith, and how baptism makes a difference in his or her expression of faith today. The interview process provides a way for the mentor to tell his or her faith story in a fun format.

3. Review a Worship Bulletin or Order of Worship

We should not assume that our youth know all the parts of a worship service, why they are important, and what each part means. The mentor is to use a worship bulletin and review the order of the worship service to make sure the youth understands all parts of the service. The model of praise, word, table, and dismissal is a simple way to explain the four major parts of how we worship God and celebrate as a community of faith. If youth have a better grasp of worship, there will be a deeper appreciation and engagement in the service in praising God.

4. Review the Church Budget

It is often said the church is always asking for money. The offering is a vital and powerful witness of a church community. Youth need to know that if everyone put only five dollars in the plate, we would not be able to offer church ministries or help people in need the way we hope. Reviewing a church budget lets young people see on paper all that is needed to fulfill the dreams and hopes of the congregation. Budgets normally include four key areas: outreach, church ministries, staff, and property care. A church budget to cover the four categories in living out its vision or ministry. Youth need to see how much money it takes to operate the church in serving Christ.

5. Allow Youth to Attend Your Place of Work or Organization in which You Volunteer

There needs to be a balance of activities done at the church and away from the church. It is helpful for the mentored youth to see the mentor in his or her natural vocational or volunteer settings. The youth will have a curiosity about what you do away from church functions. Share with him or her how your faith is expressed in your daily work or sharing time with others. If you are retired, take your youth to where you give of your time at a nonprofit organization, hobby or interest group, or even a club or social organization of which you are a part (Rotary or Kiwanis).

6. Share in a Servant Activity Together

A final activity to share together is a service project of some kind. Serve God together. Model what it means to embody the phrase, "Where two or three are gathered…" Make a difference in the local community as representatives of the church. This gives the youth a chance to show compassion toward others, see how the church is to be a witness to those in need, and develop a more meaningful relationship with the mentor. Uniting in Christ to serve gives a common story the two of you will share when having future conversations.

Auxiliary Functions

1. Gift for Youth Being Baptized

A mentor is encouraged to purchase a gift if his or her youth is being baptized at the end of the program. The gift is a symbol of celebration for the youth making such an important choice that will be life-changing. He or she is beginning a journey with Christ that will enrich that youth's life forever. Some sample gifts that could be given include a necklace with a cross, special book of faith, memorabilia piece that has a special meaning between the mentor and youth, or a baptism card of celebration.

I encourage the church to give Bibles to the youth as symbols of faith and books of strength as the youth begin their formal journey in the Christian faith.

2. Aiding the Youth on the Day of His of Her Baptism

A youth's baptism is a significant day in his or her life. Encourage family and special friends to come and celebrate the day in worship together. Mentors can assist on this day by helping behind the scenes to make sure all the youth are where they need to be. Youth are typically nervous just before their baptisms. Familiar faces and loving presences can help reduce their anxiety. Mentors can also help them get to the dressing room and make sure they return to worship in a timely manner before communion is served. This will be their first communion as baptized persons in Christ. The mentor's help on this day allows the parents and family to remain in the sanctuary to witness and celebrate the day without worrying about other details.

Mentor Letter of Thank You

Dear _____,

I am grateful that you agreed to serve as a mentor for _____ _____. Learning about baptism and becoming disciples of Jesus is an important time in the lives of our youth. As you help guide and love *him/her* during *his/her* time in this program, you will also be rewarded. *He/she* will become a true blessing in your life.

I have included the mentor expectations and mentor rationale sheets to ensure a quality experience. Please contact me if you have any questions about the process or specific activities to be fulfilled.

The weekly sitting and shadowing in worship is to begin this coming Sunday. Remember, _____(*youth's name*) will follow you wherever you go (praying at the table, reading scripture, singing the anthem, passing the offering plates, etc.). I want *him/her* to get a feel for the leadership aspects of worship. If you want to include *him/her* in those functions, feel free to find ways for *him/her* to participate.

Other details to review with you are:

- Share meals with your youth when it works out in your schedule (lunch after church, Saturday lunch, weekday evening)
- I will get you a copy of the church budget to review with your youth
- The interview sheets will be given to the youth about halfway through the program and *he/she* will ask to interview you

I have also included a schedule of our sessions from beginning to end. I want you to know the topics we will be learning about throughout the program. Please call if you want additional details about these topics. The mentor relationship will formally conclude on the Sunday we baptize the youth who make this decision.

Mentor relationships change lives. Jesus mentored twelve men into being his disciples. The world has never been the same. We all have gifts and love to share with the young people of our church. Share yourself and God will take care of the rest.

In Christ,

Appendix E: Retreat Materials

Retreat Worship Experience

Find a place in the sanctuary where you feel closest to God. Don't go any farther until you find that place. Make sure you have a Bible to guide you through the exercise.

First, take a look at the light on the communion table. The light tells us that God's presence is in this room. Say a short prayer giving thanks to God for always being with us and guiding us every day.

Second, open your Bible to the following New Testament reading: Matthew 7:24–27

When you think of this story of the wise and foolish builders, what are three things you can think of that make for a strong house to make it through a storm?

1.

2.

3.

Why did one of the houses in the story fall down and collapse?

If you think of your faith like a house, name three things you need as a Christian to help you every day of your life.

1.

2.

3.

If you look back at verse 24 of the Bible reading, there are two key verbs in this verse that help us understand what it means to be a faithful follower of God and Jesus.

Everyone then who _____ these words of mine and _____

_____

How you do you think God wants you to hear or listen as a Christian? Name three ways you are to listen.

1.

2.

3.

How do you think God wants you to act as a Christian? Name three ways you can act or share your faith with others.

1.

2.

3.

Next, how do you think your life will be different because of your baptism? How does your baptism invite you to be a new person?

Finally, say a prayer to God asking for God's help and support to be a faithful follower of Jesus. Share with God what you are thankful for in your life. Ask God to help you have a faith that is strong like the wise man who built his house on the rock.

Appendix F: Worship Materials

Sample Order of Worship for Pentecost Sunday

Prelude—A time for silent meditation

Welcome, Announcements

We Gather God's People

Hymn: "O for a Thousand Tongues to Sing" (*Chalice Hymnal, no.* 5)

Responsive Call to Worship

> Leader: May the flames of the Holy Spirit cause our hearts to warm.
> **People: Come, Holy Spirit, Come.**
> Leader: May the wind of Pentecost blow right to our souls.
> **People: Come, Holy Spirit, Come.**
> Leader: May the tongue of the Spirit give your faith a new voice.
> **People: Come, Holy Spirit, Come.**
> Leader: May you see visions, dream dreams, and sense God around you.
> **People: Come, Holy Spirit, Come.**

Hymn: "On Pentecost They Gathered" (*Chalice Hymnal, no.* 237)

Scripture Reading

Hymn: "Water, River, Spirit, Grace" (*Chalice Hymnal, no.* 366)

Service of Baptism (candidates are introduced and baptized)

Baptismal Anthem

Children's Sermon

Hymn: "Breathe on Me, Breath of God" (*Chalice Hymnal, no.* 254)

We Hear God's Word

Call to Prayer

Leader: The Spirit of God is being poured out upon us.
People: We receive this gift as we lift our hearts to God.
Leader: We pray for a spirit of empowerment.
People: We pray for a spirit of renewal and forgiveness.
Leader: Let us enter in prayer with silence.

Pastoral Prayer and Lord's Prayer

Anthem

Scripture Readings: Acts 2:1–6, 37–42; Ephesians 5:8–14

Sermon "Word, Water, Wine, and Bread"

We Come to God's Table

Hymn: "Sweet, Sweet Spirit" (*Chalice Hymnal*, #261)

Offering Meditation

Offertory

Doxology

Prayer of Dedication

Communion Meditation

Hymn: "Come, Share the Lord" (*Chalice Hymnal*, no. 408)

Prayer for the Elements

Words of Institution

Sharing the Bread and Cup

We Go Forth as God's People

Confirmation of Baptismal Candidate(s) (See Insert below)

Hymn: "We Call Ourselves Disciples" (*Chalice Hymnal*, no. 357)

Benediction

Postlude

Confirmation of Baptismal Candidate(s)

Minister: These members of the family of Christ who were baptized by water and the Holy Spirit come now to confirm their faith, declare promises, and enter the journey of discipleship. Each of you now shares our life in Christ. You have made a commitment in the act of baptism to let Christ be the Lord of your life. Baptism is not an end but a beginning. Each of you will continually live into this moment of baptism. You have also been nourished through communion at the Lord's table. Do you affirm your baptismal covenant?

Candidates: I do.

Minister: Do you commit yourself to Christ's service living with faithfulness to the church and world?

Candidates: I do.

Minister: Please respond by reading the promise and covenant of your baptism.

Candidates: I have risen from the water of baptism. I will become a witness for God. I will be a faithful follower of Jesus Christ. I receive the Holy Spirit to be with me at all times. I will be a part of the living church, the body of Christ.

Minister: May the spiritual leaders of our church now stand and give words of support and love.

Elders: We promise to pray for you, to seek the depths of faith with you, to support you,…

Deacons: and to love you. We covenant with you to love God with our heart, mind, and…

Minister: soul, and to love you as ourselves.

Minister: Will the congregation now stand and give support to the newly baptized?

Congregation: We rejoice in God's empowering love, freely given to all through grace. We welcome you, newly baptized, into the circle of love that is Christ's church. We praise God for the gifts of ministry that you bring to this community of faith and the church universal.

Minister: Let us say together the Disciples of Christ Affirmation of Faith.

All: As members of the Christian Church, we confess that Jesus is the Christ, the Son of the living God, and proclaim him Lord and Savior of the world. In Christ's name and by his grace we accept our mission of witness and service to all people. We rejoice in God, maker of heaven and earth, and in the covenant of love, which binds us to God and one another. Through baptism into Christ we enter into newness of life and are made one with the whole people of God. In the communion of the Holy Spirit we are joined together in discipleship and in obedience to Christ. At the table of the Lord we celebrate with thanksgiving the saving acts and presence of Christ. Within the universal church, we receive the gift of ministry and the light of scripture. In the bonds of Christian faith we yield ourselves to God that we may serve the One whose kingdom has no end. Blessing, glory, and honor be to God forever. Amen. [*Preamble to the Design of the Christian Church (Disciples of Christ)*]

Sharing from the Mentors

(Invite the mentors of the baptized youth to come forward and stand beside them. Ask each of them to share what it meant to be a mentor and a word about the youth he or she worked with.)

Sharing of Gifts with the Baptismal Candidates

(This is a time for the minister and key leaders to share with each candidate gifts from the church to celebrate this day of baptism. Gifts can include the baptismal certificate, Bible, special symbol of faith in the church, or other gifts appropriate for the occasion.)

Minister's Prayer of Blessing

God of holy wind and transforming waters, we celebrate the gift of baptism and what this event will mean to these young people for the remainder of their lives. We also know they are welcomed into your eternal family. Bless them and bless us as we seek to be faithful followers of your Son, Jesus Christ. Guide us and love us into the future with hope and peace. We pray in the name of Jesus Christ. Amen.

www.ingramcontent.com/pod-product-compliance
Lightning Source LLC
Chambersburg PA
CBHW081332090426
42737CB00017B/3111